Spill the Tea on Meditation

A beginner's guide to mindfulness, healing, meditation, and feeling your best self in the world of tea

by

MAUREEN LOWDEN

◆ FriesenPress

One Printers Way
Altona, MB R0G 0B0
Canada

www.friesenpress.com

Copyright © 2024 by Maureen Lowden
First Edition — 2024

All rights reserved.

No part of this publication may be reproduced in any form, or by any means, electronic or mechanical, including photocopying, recording, or any information browsing, storage, or retrieval system, without permission in writing from FriesenPress.

ISBN
978-1-03-917826-7 (Hardcover)
978-1-03-917825-0 (Paperback)
978-1-03-917827-4 (eBook)

1. BODY, MIND & SPIRIT, MINDFULNESS & MEDITATION

Distributed to the trade by The Ingram Book Company

The information and suggestions in this book are presented as topics of interest and are not intended to replace the recommendations of a qualified health professional. Any application of information, suggestions, preparations, or procedures is at the risk of the reader and any adverse effects or consequences are the reader's sole responsibility.

Recipe cooking times, product suggestions, and measurements are approximate. The product outcome is the responsibility of the individual to ascertain accuracy and quality.

Table of Contents

Dedication	vii
What's Inside	x
Prayer	1
Tea, Herbs & Meditation	2
A Cup of Tea to Pause and Experience the Moment	4
Preparing Tea in a Teapot	11
Scones	14
Words Have Meaning: A Way to Start and End Your Day	16
Meditation with Earl Grey	19
Meditation with Chamomile	41
Meditation with Lavender	59
Meditation with Butterfly-Pea Flower	81
Meditation with Matcha and Green Tea	98
Meditation with Dandelions and Pineapples	115
Meditation with Calendula and Mint	135
Meditation with Maple	155

Major Chakra Centres	172
Mudras	194
Healing Effects of Tea	198
Healing Effects of Meditation	200
The Tea Families	202
A Morning Routine	205
An Evening Routine	206
Life Loves Me	209
Mindful Awareness	211
Accommodating the Water - A Taoist Parable	212
Wrapping It Up	213
31 Days of Meditation	215
Acknowledgements	217
Books, teachers, and references	220
Photo Credits	221
Art Graphics	221

Dedication

This book is dedicated to all those struggling with questions, have a desire to draw closer to Divine consciousness, seek to rejoin life, and reignite passions. My gratitude to the thousands of years of teaching masters who have been teaching and are helping and caring for people.

I encourage you to journal any thoughts, desires, wants, or dreams in this book and to use your journaling, the poems, the meditations, the stories, and a relaxing cup of tea to help guide you to see your strengths and magnificence. Pause to think about the questions that have been provided as well as any questions that come to you as thoughts and reflect on the answers. This book is simply one person's understanding of the interconnectedness of Tea & MEditation. You are here to experience the abundance and beauty of life on this planet. Slow down and savour the moment.

As you explore your spiritual pathway, I have included a monthly chart for your use. Use the chart to benefit your spiritual practice. Mark off the days when you are able to include mindful meditation in your daily routine. Do not feel burdened by the practices of meditation. Cherish the moment. We are all not called to be a yogi practitioner or guru.

Be curious.

Explore and reflect on who you are and where the joy is in your life.

Engage in your healing journey.

Be positive. Your first thought in the morning and your last thought at night should be one of joy. You are continuously being made new – every day, every minute.

Embrace the moment. Now.

Let go of what is not serving or helping you to become your best self.

Learning is a lifetime journey that began with my first breath and will end with my last breath. To me, learning is akin to experiencing the four seasons—winter, spring, summer, and fall. Each season has its struggles. Each season has its own beauty and each season is continuously being made new.

A yoga instructor when I was in my 20s offered some wise advice. She said to learn from every experience — take what is good and what you can use to help yourself and others, and leave the rest. She helped me move beyond my anger and frustration. I believe that in loving myself, I will come closer to knowing my purpose and the Divine creator; and that letting go means to *let go of the unknown and to let go of thoughts, feelings, and emotions that are not helping me become the best version of myself.* It seems that some of my greatest challenges arise from attachment. Let go of trying to control the outcome. Let go of the negative thoughts, the negative memories, and the negative experiences. Let go of attachments. Focus on a daily affirmation, i.e., *"I love myself. Life loves me."* Letting go in any area of life requires a deep trust in the Divine consciousness. The Divine hears you, so *Love Yourself.* It is in loving yourself that you are able to love others and loving yourself will help you grow closer to the Divine.

Allow yourself five minutes of reflection time a day. Envision a rose in full bloom. See the many petals as your life experience. Focus on the centre of the rose and see its vibrant beauty. What colour is the rose? What feelings or thoughts does the rose arouse in you? Perhaps another flower is more meaningful. Envision how the flower grew from a seed and its journey through transformation. When you take the time to reflect, you will begin to notice changes in yourself. Maybe it is time for you to engage with life. Maybe your stories are similar to my stories. What does not work for you, leave it, walk away, and let go.

Dedication

Pour yourself a delightfully hot cup of tea, relax, and enjoy. ***There is always time for tea ... and meditation.***

The light and love within us creates miracles and illuminates truth.

> *Breathe. Love. Service. Sacrifice.*
>
> *The road to success is always under construction.*

What's Inside

I hope this book of short meditations, poems, personal reflections, teas to soothe your soul, recipes, and notes about herbs and plants helps you on your spiritual journey.

I was motivated to write this book, *Spill the Tea on Meditation*, to help me through the maze of meditation and spiritual jargon and to come to know myself just a little better. I love learning and I am continuously increasing my knowledge about Tea & MEditation. I am not a tea master, just someone who loves afternoon tea. I was inspired to share my personal reflections about the connection I envision between a cup of Tea & MEditation. The whole experience tells a story. It is part of my story.

Signs and synchronicity guide me daily. Perhaps you see signs that are meaningful in your life. Sometimes I listen to my inner voice, and sometimes it seems I do not listen. One thought that has remained with me is that if I do not listen, the path appears to be more difficult. It may not be more difficult, it just seems to be, so I meditate, listen to healing music, find the good in the situation, and sip a cup of tea to understand the road I am travelling on just a little better. I then see my journey take a magical turn and see abundance in my life.

> *Your task is not to seek for love, but merely to seek and find all the barriers within yourself that you have built against it.*
>
> Rumi

Prayer

Listening
Waiting
In prayer
To hear
My why
My purpose

To see and witness
The movement of God in my journey
To feel
To sense my emotions and not be upset

When I am of the world without reflection
Without consciousness
My actions and thoughts become
angry, spiteful, sad, depressed, dark, happy, jealous, surprised

When I'm in the world of spirit
I am conscious. Co-creating with Spirit
I experience the gifts of God
understanding, calm, acceptance, tolerance, patience, joy, love

I pop in and out of both worlds
My purpose
is to accept both worlds
All worlds
To create with my creator a life on earth

To listen and wait
To hear and do

Maureen Lowden

Tea, Herbs & Meditation

Tea

> There are many teas, but there is only one plant.
>
> There are many "you's", but only one "I."
>
> In your lifetime, on this planet, you have one body, one mind, and one soul to learn your purpose and to discover your gifts.
>
> Where are you? Here
>
> What time is it? Now

The camellia sinensis is the plant that is used in making tea. The leaves that sprout from the very top of this plant are transformed into different types of tea—black, green, oolong, white, etc. The teas made from these leaves contain caffeine, in varying amounts. The tea's character depends on the weather, soil, climate, and elevation, as well as how the leaves are picked from the branches and treated. Still, only one plant makes many teas. The bush is an evergreen shrub and may grow as tall as sixty feet. When it is cultivated for harvest, the tea bush is pruned to about three feet. Tea is indigenous to China, Tibet, and northern India; however, it has been transplanted and cultivated throughout the planet.

Herbs

Herbs are generally friendly but should be chosen wisely as not all herbs are friendly and some can be dangerous. Herbal teas are also known as infusions. The camellia sinensis leaves are not the source of herbal teas. An herb can be defined as a plant without woody stems and the leaves, stems, and flowers have aromatic and medicinal properties.

Herbs, like tea leaves, have the ability to lift our spirits, relax our nature, relieve stress, heal ailments, and mend our wounds, both physical and spiritual. Some herbs can be enjoyed in their unblended forms, while others, such as valerian, have a bitter taste and require the addition of other herbs and spices to make an enjoyable drink.

Mindful Meditation

Meditation can mean different things to different people. What we aim for or what we want to achieve through meditation can be many things. Mindful meditation may help with anxiety and improve your well-being. Meditation may help to improve your patience and reaction time. It may also help to relieve stress and anxiety, and energize your body and mind. Meditation may help with communication and relationships. Meditation, I believe, will help you come to know you are not the labels the physical and cultural worlds have assigned to you. You are a co-creator. You are abundance. You are awareness and consciousness. You are not ego. You are not your thoughts. Rarely do we spend time in the present moment and make authentic connections. Meditation will help you become aware of your authentic self and help you go beyond your thoughts and access a field of infinite possibilities. Cosmic consciousness goes beyond thought, and beyond the physical world. Spend some time to go within and discover your authentic self.

A Cup of Tea to Pause and Experience the Moment

There's always time for tea. That's part of my favourite saying. The whole saying is, "As the world is falling around you, there is always time for tea." I think of the men in the trenches in the world wars and how a cup of tea brought memories of home to mind. In the movies, you can see a change in the actor's face and, for just a moment, they were home.

> **As the world is falling around you, there is always time for tea.**

When you are enjoying a cup of tea and conversation with someone, for a few moments, you may experience 'home.' Home symbolically is a safe place, comfort, a place where you can share your feelings and not be judged, and where you can enjoy the present moment.

There is no problem in the world that cannot be solved when you are enjoying a cup of tea, especially …

The conversation about whether milk is poured into the teacup first or the tea is poured first and then milk is added.

How many spoonfuls of sugar are okay? A spoonful? Two spoonfuls? Or are you inclined to enjoy more?

What type of sugar is best? Is it granular white sugar, sugar cubes, Demerara sugar, brown sugar, or no sugar?

Do you drink your tea with milk or cream? What type of beverage do you choose to add, e.g., almond, oat, soy, goat, cow, pasteurized or unpasteurized?

What type of tea is best? Loose leaf, tea bags, matcha, black, oolong, green, white, yellow, Pu-erh, rooibos, Earl Grey, Darjeeling, mate, hibiscus, sencha, Assam, peppermint, jasmine, Ceylon, English breakfast or a tea blend.

Do you choose a brand name tea?

Will you use a tea strainer?

Is coffee your preferred drink or is it a hot, delicious cup of tea?

I remember my grandmother used a drip stopper on the spout of her teapot and a tea cozy to keep the tea warm.

Should you leave the tea bag in or do you give it a quick dunk and then take the tea bag out?

How long will you steep the tea? Three minutes? Five minutes? Shorter or longer?

Are you going to use the tea bag again or only use it once? Will you leave the used tea bag on the spoon, a plate, or in a bowl?

Do you recycle the used tea leaves for your plants or do you toss them out?

How big is your tea cup? Is it your favourite? Are you going to use a fine bone china teacup or a mug?

Will you have your tea with a slice of lemon?

Do you take your tea dark or light?

Is the water filtered or straight from the tap?

What teapot will you use? Will it be fine bone china, a Brown Betty, clay, or stainless steel?

Will you use a linen tablecloth? Will you have a sweet or savoury bite to eat with your tea?

Tea is not just tea.

Tea is not just tea. Water plays an important part in the making of a pot of tea and is vital for life. The average human body is more than 60% water. It is said that our thoughts, words, feelings, and emotions influence water molecules. Imagine the influence we have on our body and health with our thoughts, words, feelings, and emotions. We need to become brave, grateful, and love fully to live in joy on this planet.

5

The Japanese tea ceremony usually involves the ceremonial preparation of matcha, a green powdered tea. It is said thousands of years ago, Japanese monks travelled to China to study Buddhism and returned with tea. The purpose of the tea ceremony for the monks was a way to attain enlightenment. In today's busy culture, the tea ceremony is to bring harmony, calmness, an inner personal peace to quiet the surroundings, and to take a break from the outside world.

Many people climb Mount Hua in China to enjoy the best cup of tea at the Huashan Teahouse. While I have not made the climb, I think the best tea is served right in your own special place called home.

> *Tea may symbolically represent freedom, pleasure, extravagance, and even treasure.*

From Imperial China to Britain, the history of tea is fascinating to explore. Its history includes the rivalry between the English and the American tea traders, smugglers, murders, the Boston Tea Party, Clipper races, debates of its health-giving properties, the rise of the tea bag, and the role tea played in boosting the morale of the troops in the world wars. The British have enjoyed tea since it arrived in Britain around the mid 1600s. Britain's working class probably began drinking tea close to the middle of the 18th century when it was no longer kept under lock and key. The tradition of the 'tea break' during a working day was allowed. From there, it was not long before it became known as "afternoon tea."

I remember a friend in London, England, woke me up in the morning with a cup of tea. Late afternoon we had tea served in china cups poured from a Royal Albert teapot with fancy sandwiches, tiny desserts, and scones with jam and whipped cream. This is the deliciousness of a High Tea afternoon. I could envision the ladies sitting with their long dresses, hats, and gloves navigating the handle of the tea cup with their three fingers, thumb, and the fifth digit or pinky finger held out so as not to interfere with the delicate balance.

My mother would bring my sister and me to fancy tea parties with the women veterans, to baby and wedding showers, and to strawberry social teas where only the hostess was allowed to pour the tea. This is where I got my love of High Tea with fancy teacups, mini sandwiches, and petits fours. I introduced my daughter and my grandchildren to afternoon tea as I believe this is a special time to share with friends and family.

While writing this book, I asked friends if they drank tea and if they had special memories. All of my friends remembered having tea with their loved ones. Their faces relaxed as they told their stories, enjoying the memories of home, and how tea was served. Become aware of your senses when you are enjoying a cup of tea. What are you thinking about when you pour the boiling water into the tea pot and carefully place the teabag? Do you smell the delicate aroma of the leaves? Do you feel the warmth of your cup? Do you see the tea leaves unfurling? Sight, sound, smell, touch, and taste may all convey a message to us. We are capable of sensing much more than our five senses. We may no longer be unconscious of what is before us and experience consciousness in the moment. We can transition from the busyness of the outside world to a quiet and comfortable space. What rituals and memories have become parts of your tea story?

Your intention and your presence when pouring a cup of tea is important. Tea can help hydrate and quench your thirst. Matcha can help stabilize and energize you. Peppermint tea can help with digestion. Chia arouses the senses with the aroma of cinnamon and other spices. A cup of tea should not be a drink you bought in the drive-through on your way to somewhere. It is not about pouring hot water over a tea bag, allowing you to continue on with your busy life. It should be a ritual that arouses your senses, creates space for you for reflection and mindfulness, and brings a feeling of calmness. Once you realize a cup of tea is about relaxation, balance, and harmony, I think you will begin to see the importance of the preparation and taking a break from the outside world. By simply focusing on the moments of preparing and serving tea, for yourself or for others, you will begin to realize the interconnectedness of life.

Tea masters will refer to the finest spring waters, the ideal temperatures for brewing, the ideal environment for growing, the finest leaves, the finest taste, and the finest vessel to hold tea and to drink it. Tea may symbolically represent freedom, pleasure, extravagance, and even treasure. Tea connects people.

Meditation is also about connecting – connecting with oneself and with others. The practice of meditation can be a solitary practice or one with two or more people. Meditation helps us to become aware of the present moment. It may help us to relax, become more patient, and have a better understanding of knowing when it is time to let go of the past and enjoy the present moment. Meditation and tea are connected, partnering to bring about a sacred and reflective moment.

Mindful meditation can be as simple as sitting or lying down and focusing on your breath, a word, a phrase, an object, or silence. Mindful meditation can be about doing and can include your job, a project you are working on, and even reading a book. Setting your intention is what is important. Bring the focus to your intention and then softly let the thought go. Let go of your expectations. Let go of the outcome. Let go of judging yourself and others. Change the negative narrative into a learning experience. Begin the transformation process.

Pay attention to your feelings, what you sense, what you are doing, and when you are helping others. It is always a good practice to ground yourself and clear any negativity before you start your day and before you begin meditation.

Grounding is simply being in the present moment where negative energy can be released. Grounding is the process of balancing your emotional, mental, physical, and energy states and releasing any negative thoughts and feelings.

There are many breathing techniques to help focus and ground you. Try this one. Place your hand on your heart centre. Connect to your breath, feel the rise and fall of your chest, take in a few deep breaths, and focus on the rhythmic flow. Breathe using the count of four-two-four: breathe in through your nose for a count of four, pause for two, and breathe out through your mouth, making a sigh, for a count of four and pause for two before your next inhale. Repeat two times or more. Do what is comfortable. A few deep breaths may be beneficial. You may experience a state of calm and relaxation.

Before you begin your meditation, reflect on questions that may be important to you or questions that will help in seeking joy in your life. As you ask yourself questions where you are seeking an answer, allow the answers to come to you. It doesn't matter what or if any answers come immediately for, as they arrive, let the answers go. Let them float away into the cosmos and bring your focus back to your breath. Meditation is a time of self-reflection and learning.

Remember: As the world is falling around you, there is always time for tea ... and meditation.

True or False

Tea is the 2ⁿᵈ most popular drink after water.

Drinking tea aids decision-making in the work place.

Tea breaks have been around for over 200 years.

There are over 1500 types of tea including white, green, oolong, and black tea.

Preparing Tea in a Teapot

The magic formula to prepare a pot of tea is usually 1:1 - one heaping teaspoon (5 ml) of loose-leaf tea and one cup (250 ml) of water boiled to a certain temperature. The correct temperature for a particular type of tea varies. You will find accurate temperatures in various books about tea. Some tea kettles will also provide instruction for the correct water temperature, e.g., my kettle lists green and white tea at 175°F (79°C), oolong at 195°F (90°C), French press at 200°F (93°C), black and herbal at 205°F (96°C). Water quality and water temperature are important.

- ✓ Begin by choosing your favourite teacup, teapot, and your favourite tea leaves. Get everything ready (milk, spoon, sugar, lemon, etc.) so you will be able to follow though with purpose. Be aware that boiling water will scald the tea leaves and destroy the delicate aroma.

- ✓ Warm the teapot with hot water, wait approximately thirty seconds to one minute, and then discard.

- ✓ Add the boiling water and tea leaves. There are many ways to prepare tea leaves: (a) Fill the tea pot with boiling water, place the tea leaves loosely in the teapot, and when ready use a strainer to pour the tea. (b) Place the tea leaves into a tea strainer or ball, fill the teapot with boiling water, place the strainer into your teapot, and pour when ready. If you are using a tea strainer, make sure the tea leaves are not cramped and that there is enough space for the tea leaves to unfurl. (c) Place the tea leaves into a tea bag, gently tie the bag to hold the leaves in, fill the teapot with boiling water, place the tea bag into your teapot, and pour when ready.

- ✓ Let the tea leaves infuse for several minutes depending upon the type of tea you choose.

- ✓ Stop the infusion process by pouring the tea (using a strainer for loose tea leaves) into another teapot or cup or by removing the strainer or tea bag. If the infusion process is too short, the delicate leaves will not reveal their true characteristics and aroma. If the process is too long, you will begin to taste the bitterness of the tannins.

Morning Tea Meditation

Make yourself a cup of tea and find a quiet space where you will not be disturbed for the next few minutes. Maybe the children are running around or have joined you at the table and you feel you cannot be separated. If you are driving a car, you should pull over in a safe place and stop the engine. If a quiet and safe space is not available, whatever is happening around you, accept it, and breathe.

For this meditation you may wish to keep your eyes open and your senses aware of your environment. You are simply going to shift your awareness. Notice how your body is feeling right now. Do you feel relaxed or rushed? What do you see? Become aware of your surroundings and give thanks for this present moment and for everything and everyone in it. Now shift your awareness to your cup of tea. Begin to wrap your fingers around the cup of tea and feel the warmth. Maybe

Preparing Tea in a Teapot

you have made an iced tea. Feel the coolness of the glass and breathe in the moment. Bring the cup closer to your nose and inhale the aroma. Take a sip and enjoy the deliciousness of the tea. Become mindful of what you are doing. Feel the tea touching your lips, flowing over your tongue, down your throat, and through your body. Take a breath in and exhale, continue to sip your tea and savour its delicate flavour. Become aware of how your hands and arms are moving and how your senses are reacting. Breathe in and become mindful of your cup of tea. Breathe out and feel your body relax. Rest in these few moments of mindful awareness.

Namaste.

Scones

Scones are a favourite with High Tea. For me, the scones are best when they are served warm with whipped butter, whipping cream, strawberry jam, and fruit.

Ingredients

4 cups (960 g) flour
2 teaspoons (10 ml) salt
6 teaspoons (30 ml) baking powder
½ cup (125 g) sugar (plus 2 tablespoons optional)
1 egg (room temperature and beaten)
2 cups (500 ml) milk or buttermilk or beverage of your choice (room temperature)
¾ cup (190 g) butter (room temperature)

Optional: 1 cup (250 g) dried fruit, e.g., dried currants, dried cranberries, raisins, etc.

Method

Mix the dry ingredients (flour, salt, baking powder, sugar) together minus 2 tablespoons of sugar. Optional: add dried fruit.
Add the butter using a pastry blender or two knives to cut the butter into the dry ingredients. The mixture should be slightly lumpy.
In a separate bowl or mixing bowl, beat one egg. Add in 2 cups (500 ml) of milk (or beverage of your choice).
Pour the egg and milk mixture into the dry ingredients and mix until dough is combined. Let stand for approximately one minute.

Scones

Place the dough onto a floured surface and knead the dough until you have a smooth ball of dough. If the dough is sticky, sprinkle it lightly with flour. If it is too dry, add a few drops of milk or water.
Cut the ball of dough in half. Working with one half of the dough—roll out onto a floured surface until about 1 inch (2.5 cm) thick. Cut the dough into rounds or triangles.

If you need to save time and you don't want to knead the dough, place a large spoonful of dough onto the cookie sheet. The scones will look uneven but they are just as tasty.

Place the dough on a parchment lined cookie sheet.
Preheat oven to 425°F (220°C) and bake for about 16-18 minutes until the scones are lightly browned on the bottom. While the scones are still warm sprinkle the top with the 2 tablespoons of sugar.
Serve warm with butter, jam, and a hot cup of tea.

Words Have Meaning: A Way to Start and End Your Day

Chakra

What is a Chakra? The word chakra in Sanskrit means *wheel*, and generally refers to energy points in the body or wheels of life. These energy wheels are similar to acupuncture points in the body and should be open and balanced so energy can move freely throughout the body. The chakras correspond to bundles of nerves, major organs, and areas of our body that affect our emotional and physical well-being. Energy circulates throughout the body and travels along invisible pathways. When our energy wheels are balanced, our body and mind functions better. One way to open and align the energy points in your body is to breathe in ten deep breaths when you wake up and again in the evening before you fall asleep.

Journal

Why journal? Journaling is a form of meditation or prayer. It is a way to connect to your higher self. Journaling helps you to listen to your intuitive self as well as to the Divine, God, Creator, Great Spirit or any name you give to your higher power. Start by putting thoughts on paper. Sometimes, I draw in my journal. I might draw an insect or an animal that presented itself to me, or it may be still life. Whatever inspires you to put pencil or pen to paper, that's journaling. Write about your feelings, your thoughts, or what comforts you. "Habit stack" your journaling practice. Habit stack is when you connect a new habit to a daily habit to remind you to do something. Perhaps when you have your morning drink you will be reminded to pick up your pen and jot down whatever comes to mind. Writing, drawing, and using your hands will engage your body and your mind. Using your hands will help with learning, improve creativity, and can help you solve problems. Start now and enjoy the miracles created by your hands.

Routine
Establish a routine. Routines help to reduce stress and anxiety and can lead to a more relaxed you. Your mental health improves. You will sleep better, resulting in you making wiser decisions. A routine can be fulfilling and will bring a sense of joy as you focus on what inspires you and what motivates you. You may eat better and become more active. It is a way to kick-start your day.

In the morning, prepare your favourite tea, grab your journal, open and clear your chakra centres with a few deep breaths, put pencil to paper, and consciously sip your tea.

Meditation
Why meditate? Mindful meditation can turn your day or a simple task into so much more. Find a place to meditate where you can relax, feel safe, and be comfortable. You may choose to lie down, sit, or be in a yoga pose. You may wish to enjoy a cup of tea, eat a delicious scone, or simply focus on your breath. There is no set amount of time. You can choose to reflect for a moment, ten minutes, thirty minutes, or however much time you feel is beneficial. If you set a specific amount of time and you are interrupted, do what you need to do. You can always come back to your meditation. Meditation can help relieve stress as well as having many other health benefits. You might find you have more patience and are better able to respond to stressful situations. Meditation may help with blood pressure, sleep issues, digestion, depression, diet, and memory. Meditation may help change some of your life habits.

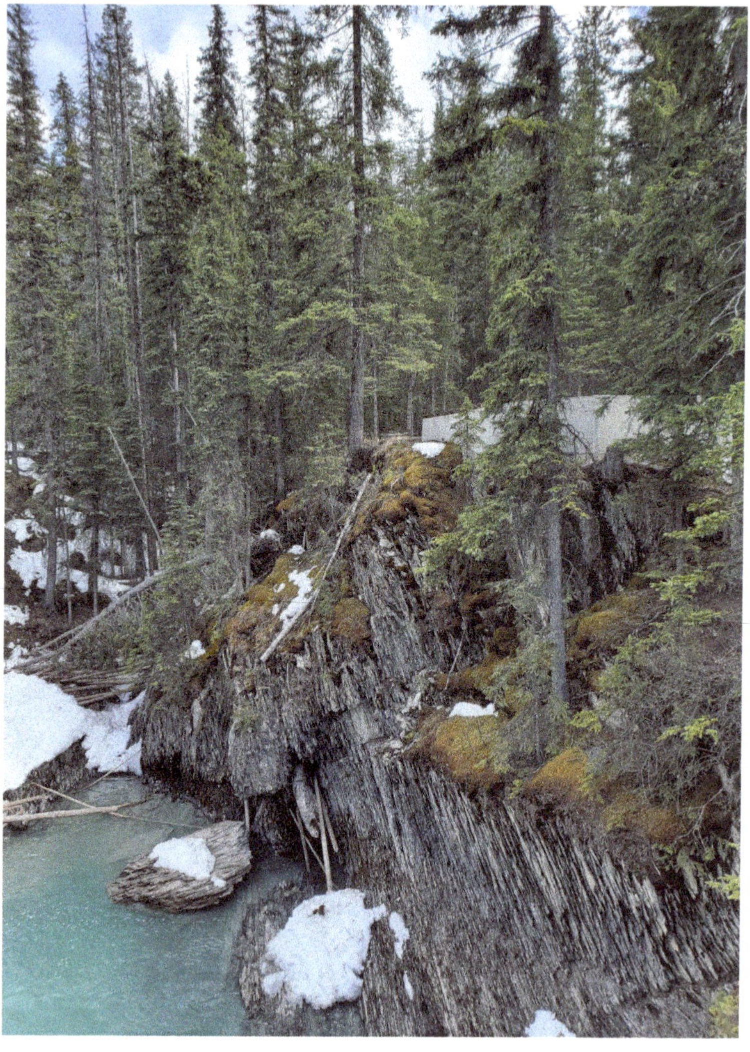

Meditation with Earl Grey

Poem

Journal Prompts & Self-Reflection Questions

Affirmations

Tea & MEditation

My Musings

Nature/Tea Focus—Earl Grey Tea

My Musings: Stories. We all have stories to tell. I believe I am a storyteller and I love to weave the family truths I hold dear into a story. The events and circumstances that shape our lives are unique to each one of us. Our stories are perceived and experienced differently. One of my stories is about being the youngest and fourth-born in the family. My brother, Gary (second-born), left this world when he was ten days old. My husband's name is Gary. My eldest grandson's name is Gary. I remember as a little girl playing a children's game in the school playground and the boy's name I was going to marry started with the letter *G*. Coincidence? Synchronicity? Our stories impact our journey. What stories have helped shaped your life?

Spill the Tea on Meditation

Feminine Wisdom

She created the heavens and earth
there was chaos and darkness
She created the sun and the moon
there was light
Yin and Yang
a becoming
She created the waters
there was order and flow
She gave birth to life
a garden
an oasis
a place to rest
to create
to give birth.
Life is about choice-
to trust an invisible higher power, or
to trust what is visible.
the duality of creation.
the chaos of
Becoming

Maureen Lowden

Journal Prompts & Self-Reflection Questions

(Use this space to journal and self-reflect)

> **Self-reflection:** Reflection opens the door to our heart. Reflection helps us to understand why the same situations occur over and over again and helps us to move and change with ease and grace. Self-reflection will help lead us to humility, helps us to release control, and helps us to understand who we really are—to think rightly about ourselves and to know that we are always learning. We can set boundaries. We can choose kindness despite the pain we have received. We can choose respect and demand better of others. When we journal we can use prompts that will help us to understand our path toward change. Do your goals reflect your deepest desire? What helps you stay focused and motivated? How quickly do you get back up when you are discouraged?

What life lessons are you grateful for?

_____

_____

_____

_____

_____

_____

_____

Who in your life are you grateful for?

___

What safeguards have you used to help you make better choices? To help you establish boundaries?

___

A professor introduced the topic of reflection and how reflection can influence our decisions. My understanding is that mindful and right thinking can help control our emotions and feelings. The Buddha said, *"We are what we think. All that we are arises with our thoughts.*

With our thoughts, we make our world." The amount of suffering and sorrow we experience is usually dependent upon our choices and our thoughts. The diagram below shows how we can make choices with reflection and without reflection. Without reflection, we act with no clear understanding of why. We act or do without thinking. To remember past events and behaviour is important; however, it is just as important to know if we are reacting from the hurt or joy of past memories, and if those memories serve a purpose in the present moment. Right thinking leads us to compassion and awareness. Awareness leads to understanding. Understanding helps us to forgive and to be grateful. We all have stories to tell. Take control of your thoughts, observe your feelings, explore why you are experiencing these feelings, slow down, focus on your breath, and create a new possibility. Create a new story.

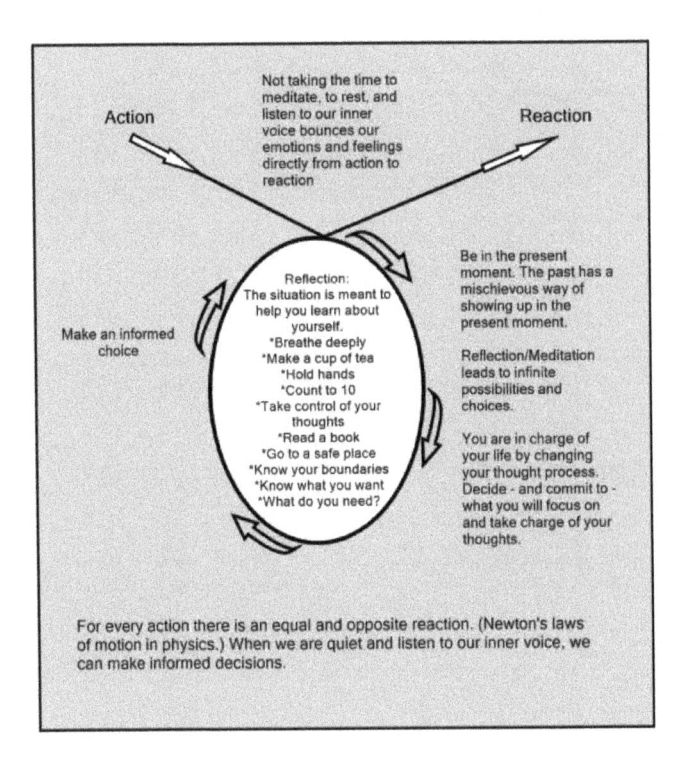

```
Action                                                              Reaction
         Not taking the time to
         meditate, to rest, and
         listen to our inner
         voice bounces our
         emotions and feelings
         directly from action to
         reaction

                    Reflection:           Be in the present
              The situation is meant to   moment. The past has a
              help you learn about        mischievous way of
                    yourself.             showing up in the
                *Breathe deeply           present moment.
Make an informed   *Make a cup of tea
    choice         *Hold hands            Reflection/Meditation
                   *Count to 10           leads to infinite
                *Take control of your     possibilities and
                     thoughts             choices.
                   *Read a book
                 *Go to a safe place      You are in charge of
               *Know your boundaries      your life by changing
                *Know what you want       your thought process.
                 *What do you need?       Decide - and commit to -
                                          what you will focus on
                                          and take charge of your
                                          thoughts.

For every action there is an equal and opposite reaction. (Newton's laws
of motion in physics.) When we are quiet and listen to our inner voice, we
can make informed decisions.
```

The journey towards personal growth is messy, chaotic, and unpredictable, and always worth it. Growth is not a linear process (as the chart may suggest) progressing from one stage to another in a series of steps. Growth is messy and chaotic but out of chaos comes order and an understanding of our strengths and weaknesses. If we can let go of our perceptions, our expectations, attachments, and memories, our understanding of events in our lives and our behaviour becomes clearer.

The Process of Growth
with Meditation

Mindful Awareness
(Being mindful of yourself in the world)

Being Comfortable with Oneself
(Awareness of the world, motivation to grow and change)

Self Awareness
(Going through change, Being open to change)

Personal Responsibility
(Self-compassion, Compassion for others)

Harmony
(Willingness to understand another person's perspective, deep caring for another, others are seen and heard)

Life Satisfaction
(Self is free of opinions and perceptions of others)

Authenticity
(Self is able to break away from the influences of the world, able to break away from the perceived demands of others)

Wisdom
(Self-govern and resolve the perceived contradictions of the self)

Affirmations

I Am

Affirmation

_____
_____
_____
_____
_____
_____

Visualization

_____
_____
_____
_____
_____

Intention / Action Plan

_____
_____
_____
_____
_____
_____

I am powerful.
I am all that I am supposed to be.
I am grateful for all the joy, abundance, and love that I receive.
I honour and respect myself and I connect to my true inner self.
My story connects me to my friends, family, community, to those I love, and to the world.
I love who I am becoming.
I am worthy of receiving love.
Every day I fall in love with myself and my journey.
I love myself and others exactly as they are.
I am strong.
I am courageous.
I respect myself and know my boundaries.
I bring my best self to every situation.

All the darkness in the world cannot extinguish the light of a single candle.

St. Francis of Assisi

Tea & MEditation

Find a place where you feel safe and comfortable. Breathe normally until you feel your body is relaxed. Take in a deep breath and exhale through your mouth with a sigh. Repeat this pattern a few more times. When you are relaxed and ready, touch your heart centre with both hands.

Ask yourself any questions you are seeking an answer for and pause between each question. What are you grateful for?

Ask yourself what is your passion? Where, in your lifetime, have you experienced joy and happiness? Be present with your joy and let it settle within you. Any answers that come to you, acknowledge them, and then let the thoughts go. Stay in the present moment, where you are relaxed and safe. With each breath and chant, feel your chest rising with every inhale and lowering with each exhale. Release any stress you are feeling in your body right now. Roll your shoulders up to your ears and down. Move your head from side to side.

Silently chant the mantra *AUM* and give attention to the silent intervals between the chants. When you are ready release the mantra and breathe at a normal pace.

Ask for support and understanding to help you walk through your struggles when the past presents itself and the future is unknown.

Seek compassion when you feel an injustice or lack of respect is being shown towards you and towards others.

When you experience doubt, ask for faith to see more clearly. Know that everything changes and is being made new.

When you experience darkness ask for the light to enter your heart so you will be able to move forward with empathy.

Seek love when you feel angry or see anger in others.

Ask for love and forgiveness. Feel a sense of calm and acknowledge forgiveness for yourself and for those who have injured you.

When you feel impatient, ask for patience. Where you feel there is sadness, ask for joy.

Know that the Divine sees your struggle. Know you are safe and supported. Your story has helped you become the incredible person you are today.

With your hands at your heart centre, visualize a glowing light. Imagine the light expanding within and throughout your being. Let the light envelop you in warmth and understanding. Golden Divine energy surrounds you and pulls you into its warmth. Rest in this warmth and understanding for as long as you wish.

Let go of any thoughts and continue to focus on your breath. You are not alone. The Divine is co-creating with you and helping you experience joy in the present moment.

When you are ready, bring your hands together in a prayer position and give thanks. Visualize the earth orbiting around the sun, feel the warmth of the sun and send this feeling of warmth and peace out to the whole world.

Hydrate. Pour yourself a cup of tea. Namaste.

(The divine light in me bows to the divine light in you.)

There is a calmness to a life lived in gratitude, a quiet joy.

Ralph H. Blum

Tea & MEditation

Start by finding a comfortable position. Close your eyes and rest your hands gently in your lap. Relax your neck and shoulders. If you feel there is some tightness, try a few shoulder rolls by lifting your shoulders up and down. Allow the area of the neck and shoulders to soften and then place your focus on the breath. Become still, allowing your breath to connect you to the moment. When you are breathing in, know you are breathing in. Breathe in deeply filling up your lungs. When you are breathing out, know you are breathing out. Push the air in your lungs out with a sigh. Make every single breath a conscious one.

When you feel safe and relaxed, breathe in for four and pause, breathe out for four and pause. Complete this cycle a few more times. If it is comfortable, make your exhale a little longer than your inhale – breathe in for four, pause, breathe out for six, and pause.

Allow your breathing to return to normal. If you are caught up in your thoughts or emotions, return your attention to your breath. Be comfortable with letting any thoughts go. Visualize your thoughts, fears, negative energy, and emotions being carried downstream in a river. Let them flow with the water. Be open to whatever is in the moment. Breathe into it.

Silently repeat the mantra *Shanti* or the word *Peace* and visualize your body being refreshed and revitalized. Stay with this mantra for a few minutes. When you are ready, let go of the mantra and return your focus to your breath. With your eyes closed, silently repeat your intentions for the day.

Meditation with Earl Grey

> I am in dynamic harmony within myself.
> My mind, body, and spirit are balanced and aligned in love.
> I embrace my intuitive and inquisitive mind with grace.
> I welcome time and space with gratitude.
> I enjoy abundance and love in my life.
> The light within me is loving and compassionate.
> I am loving and compassionate.

Gently open your eyes and move your body. Wiggle your fingers and toes. Bring your hands to your heart centre and give thanks. Send peace out to the whole world and to those you love.

Hydrate. Pour yourself a cup of tea and enjoy.

Namaste. *(The divine light in me bows to the divine light in you.)*

Note: The mantra *Shanti* is said to invoke peace and is widely used in Hinduism, Buddhism, and Jainism. The mantra is generally said three times for peace in the mind, body, and spirit; and for the past, present, and future.

*Connect your intention to something that is important to you and what will help motivate you towards your goal throughout the day.

Mistakes are the best way to understand your strengths and weaknesses, but they will bear fruit only if you acknowledge them and view them as opportunities to learn, instead of defeats.

James Van Praagh

My Musings

Every day I take my dog for a morning walk and occasionally I receive signs that help guide me throughout the day. The signs are reminders that I do not walk alone. There have been maple leaves and the maple keys falling right at my feet, a maple leaf attached to my car door, feathers, dragonflies landing beside me, a rabbit, a toad, a monarch butterfly, and a walking stick to name just a few of the signs. I have also experienced people showing up at the right time and for the right reasons.

One sign in particular I noticed on my walks was seeing a robin. For several weeks, the robin came to the park and perched on the fence beside me. I began to think this robin had a message for me. At the time, I was struggling with my reality, holding onto my path, loving myself, being content with and understanding my life choices, knowing my truth, not knowing the why, and trying to understand my current circle of life. I was once advised me that living life on this planet will include receiving with grace, giving with grace, and those who will take advantage of you and your generosity. We are living in a world where our reality is what we create. Abundance is truly meant for us and the only thing holding me back from receiving abundance is myself. What I needed to do was to hold all truths in my heart and believe that this journey will pass. This beautiful robin helped me to believe that miracles happen.

Symbolically, a robin brings hope, renewal, and rebirth. It symbolizes new beginnings, new projects, and good things to come. I am conscious of the robin's symbolic message and I feel the need to honour it as I write. I am in a transitional phase of life where everything I thought I knew to be important and stable changed. While I love family traditions, on this new journey, I realized that traditions are not that important. Traditions are choices. I made choices that greatly affected my future. I became aware of where I placed importance and what I believed was important. I was pushed into a state of fear and anxiety – a state of nothingness where my purpose was no longer evident. The robin met me every day as a symbol of hope and renewal and remained until I believed that a new beginning was possible.

Messages from Spirit are delivered to us by someone, an animal, a sound, or something else. These messages are known as cledons - messages from someone, a divine spirit, dreams, animals, or an intuitive sense that grabs your attention and helps you focus beyond the noise and the busyness of life. Today, the synchronicity of the message is sometimes referred to as nothing more than coincidence but maybe, some day, you will become aware of a connection and able to take action.

The world is changing at a pace far beyond our imagination and capacity to understand it. Throughout my life I have experienced many cledons. When my husband died, my sister sent me a song by Rita MacNeil – *Flying on Your Own*. She heard the song on the radio and it spoke to her. The message was received – there isn't anything we cannot do on our own. Throughout my university studies, I received messages whenever I questioned if I was on the right path. During a very important time in my life a friend mentioned that messages can be delivered in many ways to help us gain a better understanding of the situation that is confronting us. It is an amazing time to be alive and to see beyond what is in front of us.

Acceptance of the present moment is complicated. The path to stillness is difficult. The path to wisdom is easier said than done. For me, it was time to let go of traditions and the past. Labels are not important. The Ten Commandments are not laws, but guidance for people to help live life in wisdom and community. Life itself is a miracle. Life is love. Love is fluid, ever present, a flowing energy that permeates everything and can be accessed if we seek it. I need to trust that the universe, the Divine is listening, and will give me what I need at the right time. Perhaps my purpose is to simply enjoy life and to help others when I can. I have noticed many synchronicities or coincidences at various times in my life, and I know when I am ready, what I need to live in the moment will happen. I need to listen to hear the message.

I remember a professor sharing that it is the "mis" before a word that brings difficulty when we communicate with others. Sometimes we are misunderstood. There is miscommunication or a misunderstanding. We can be mistaken, mismanaged, and misjudged in different situations. We see the world for all it can be and for all it should be but each one of us sees the world differently. We see our life for all its blessings and yet we struggle holding on to attachments and things while walking our path. At times I feel alone and yet I know I do not walk alone. Solitude is not loneliness.

I love having a cup of Earl Grey tea, listening to the birds sing in the early morning hours and watching them fly off to explore their world or to fly home in the evening. I feel a sense of hope, calm, and appreciation for life. That is what I hope to bring in my writings for myself and for the holder of this book. On 'My Musings' pages, you are invited to read some of my life stories and I hope you will enjoy the poems I have written. This is my journey right now. My purpose.

As a way of ending my stories and meditations, I will use the salutation or greeting Namaste, which generally means *I bow to you. I respect you. The divine light in me bows to the divine light in you.*

Namaste.

Meditation with Earl Grey

Nature/Tea Focus
Earl Grey

Earl Grey tea is scented with oil of bergamot that is extracted from a small citrus fruit grown in the Mediterranean region. Like tea leaves, there are many grades of bergamot oil—some are natural and some are synthetic. The tea has a natural citrus flavour.

I came to know about Earl Grey tea on a Christmas house tour. We visited several houses to see Christmas decorating at its finest and to enjoy a food sampling. At one house we were given a sample of Earl Grey tea. A delicious hot cup of tea during a festive season. I have loved Earl Grey tea ever since.

There are many stories about Earl Grey tea. I suppose the true story is the story that you believe to be true. I love historical fiction novels and I can visualize Lord Grey returning to Britain from China around the 1800s. He truly enjoyed drinking tea. As soon as Lord Grey cleaned up his shipping business, he got off his ship and cheerfully arrived home to his wife and family. He then immediately locked up the tea in a large handmade wooden cabinet to be enjoyed only by his loyal friends and, of course, Queen Victoria. Tea was so loved by everyone that Lord Grey had the tea master create a special blend. The tea master took into consideration the environment and water and used bergamot to offset the minerals in the local water supply. Lady Grey served this tea to her many visitors and guests.

Earl Grey de la Crème is one of my favourite teas and is scented with the vibrant blue cornflower petals. There are several varieties of the cornflower plant and it is known for its medicinal and culinary properties.

Earl Grey Tea

(ratio: 1 teaspoon of (5 ml) tea leaves: 1 cup (250 ml) of boiled water)

To make Earl Grey tea, boil approximately two cups (500 ml) of water in a small saucepan or kettle. Warm the teapot with hot or warm water. After about one minute, discard the warm water from the teapot. Place two teaspoons (10 ml) of Earl Grey loose tea leaves in a teabag and gently tie the teabag or use an infuser. Once the water has boiled to the correct temperature, fill your teapot with the boiled water and add the tea leaves. Let the tea leaves steep for two to three minutes for the best flavour or longer depending on how strong you like your tea. Enjoy with your choice of milk and sweeten to taste, or you may prefer to enjoy drinking this delicious tea with no additives.

Earl Grey Spritzer

Ingredients
1/3 cup (79 ml) Earl Grey tea syrup
1/3 (79 ml) lemon soda or Prosecco
ice
mint leaves or a lemon wedge for garnish
1 or 2 Earl Grey tea bags or 2 teaspoons (15 ml) of loose tea leaves in a teabag

Simple Syrup
(Simple syrup is usually the ratio of 1:1; however, it really depends on the sweetness you prefer)
1 cup (250 ml) water
2 cup (250 g) sugar

Instructions
Simple syrup: add the water and sugar into a small saucepan. Cook on a medium heat until the sugar has dissolved. Remove from the heat. Immediately add 1 or 2 Earl Grey tea bags, steep for approximately 5 minutes, and then let cool. Strain and pour into an air tight container.

To make the spritzer, pour 3 to 4 tablespoons (45-60 ml) of Earl Grey syrup into each glass. Pour lemon soda or Prosecco to fill the glass. Garnish with a thin slice of lemon or mint leaves. If you prefer a sweeter drink, add more syrup.

Note: You can make the syrup ahead of time. After cooling, store the syrup in a glass, airtight container in the refrigerator for up to a week or more.

Earl Grey Lavender Cooler

Ingredients
- 3/4 cup (6 fl oz) Earl Grey black tea
- ¼ cup (60 ml) gin or Prosecco
- 2 tablespoon (28 ml) Lavender simple syrup* (The syrup can be made ahead of time.)
- Adjust to taste

Method
Shake all ingredients in a cocktail shaker with ice. Strain into a glass.

Lavender Simple Syrup

(Simple syrup is usually the ratio of 1:1; however, it really depends on the sweetness you prefer and the strength of lavender.)

Ingredients
2 cups (500 g) sugar
1 cup (250 ml) water
2 to 3 tablespoons (30-45 g) lavender blossoms. Use only culinary-grade lavender, fresh or dried. If you are using fresh, use the buds. Do not use the stems or the green leafy sprigs.

Method
Bring the water and sugar to a boil and stir until the sugar has dissolved.
Add the lavender buds, reduce the heat, and let simmer for approximately 3-5 minutes.
Strain into a bottle or a mason jar. When cool, cover and refrigerate.

Note: The syrup will keep for a week or more in the refrigerator in a glass, air-tight container. Simple syrup can be added to lemonade, cocktails, or wherever you would like a little taste of lavender sweetness.

The sound of your voice and the energy of your presence are as personal as your fingerprint and carries a vibrational frequency that uniquely belongs to you.

Gina Breedlove from The Vibration of Grace

Journal

We are not here to be perfect; we are here to be human.

Heidi Smith

Journal

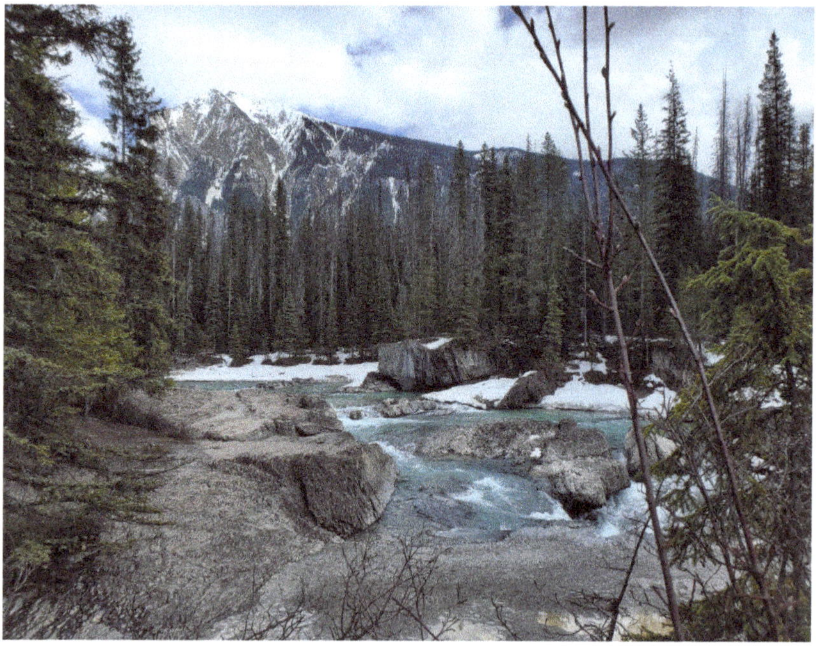

Meditation with Chamomile

Poem

Journal Prompts & Self-Reflection Questions

Affirmations

Tea & MEditation

My Musings

Nature/Tea Focus—Chamomile

Journal Prompts & Self-Reflection Questions

Take a little time for self-reflection. Ask yourself a few reflective questions: What is my purpose? What matters most to me? What do I need to let go of? If not now, then when? What am I fearful of? Grab your journal or write in this book any thoughts that come to mind. Questions will help you align your life purpose with your deepest desires.

It is time to put pen or pencil to paper.

Faith

Can you move a mountain?
I think so.
Mountains are moved by swiftly flowing waters.
Moved with the shifting tectonic plates of the earth,
nestled into one another to fit snugly until the next shift.
Mountains are reshaped by the falling rain and the melting of glaciers.
Reshaped by pathways carved out by nature and humans.
Changed by the natural spreading of seeds by animals, birds,
and insects.
Eroded by the earth's climate and changed forever.
Can you move a mountain?
I think so.
What appears to be majestic and strong can change
a little bit at a time until you recognize the mountain no more.
Time changes everything.

Maureen Lowden

Journal Prompts & Self-Reflection Questions

(Use this space to journal and self-reflect)

> **Who am I?** Looking within and reflecting upon your authentic self helps you to gain a better understanding of the words, '*You are not your thoughts.*' You are the observer and you are here to learn and to love life. To understand yourself is the greatest gift you can give to yourself. We sometimes wear a mask to hide our vulnerability, to hide our pain, to hide our confusion and lack of understanding, and even to hide our love. You are more than your name, your physical body, your attachments, job, education, family roles, beliefs, and actually anything your culture and your environment define as you. Your soul was guided to this physical world before you even existed and your soul will be guided when it is time for you to leave. Culture calls us to focus on '*we*'; but, to understand our true, authentic self, we are also called to focus on '*I*.' I Am. To love ourselves unconditionally requires the merging of our sacred feminine and divine masculine self. We are like the peacock with its beautiful plumage. There are many 'eyes' on the peacock's feathers but only one beautifully created bird. Enjoy the journey and co-create with your Higher Power.

How do I define myself?

_____

_____

_____

_____

_____

What labels do I use to define myself? To define others?

_____

_____

_____

_____

_____

_____

What label is important right now?

_____

_____

_____

_____

_____

Meditation with Chamomile

Affirmations

Love and Self-Confidence

Affirmation

_____
_____
_____
_____
_____

Visualization

_____
_____
_____
_____

Intention / Action Plan

_____
_____
_____
_____

Love is my strength and my foundation.
I am not alone.
I am love.
I am worthy.
I am the creator of my life.
I am resilient
I welcome change.
Adaptability is my strength.
I am flexible.
I am immune to destructive criticism and flattery.
I spend money wisely.
I show my true self and know that my being and doing are for the highest good of all.
I am strong.
Whatever I need will come to me now under grace and in perfect ways.
My story is my truth.
I am fulfilled.
I deserve to be happy.
I appreciate all the ways in which I am unique.
I will fulfill that which I am created to do.

Every day is a new beginning. Take a deep breath, smile, and start again.

Unknown

Tea & MEditation

Prana, the vital life energy force, is flowing through everything. It radiates within, through, and around everything and everyone in this world. Pranayama is generally understood as breath control and is one of the main components of yoga and meditation. Your breathing is influenced by your thoughts and your thoughts can be influenced by your breath. Your thoughts will not distract you when you focus on your breath. Everything is connected.

You might wish to make a cup of tea if you are seated and enjoy its delicate aroma and taste or find a comfortable position lying down where you will not be disturbed. Take a deep breath in through your nose and exhale through your mouth. Relax your shoulders, your facial muscles, and your neck. Sense within you where there is pain and send healing thoughts to this area. Allow yourself to pause and breathe as you transition away from what you were doing prior to this moment. Let go of any thoughts that come to you and return your focus to your breath. Allow your eyes to softly close.

Focusing on your breath sense the natural way your breath travels throughout the body. Notice the rise of your chest with each inhale and the release of the body on each exhale. Breathe in and out without effort and relax into this feeling. Starting with your next inhale, breathe in for a count of three and exhale for a count of three. Notice the pause between each breath. Continue this breathing pattern a few more times.

Meditation with Chamomile

When you are ready, on your next breath, lengthen your exhale by doubling the count. Inhale for three and exhale for six. Continue breathing deeply. Practise with any count that is supportive for you. There is no rush. There is no right or wrong, only what serves you today.

Remember to breathe with a pace that is comfortable and steady for you.

Visualize your breath as energy flowing to every cell, organ, and system throughout and around your body. Visualize this energy vibrating beyond your skin and out into the universe. You are connecting with the energy force and the universal consciousness.

When you are ready, release the counting and control of your breath. Rest in this space for a few moments. If you start counting again, acknowledge it, and settle into your natural flow and relaxed breathing pattern. Allow your body to rest.

As you open your eyes, give thanks and send love and healing out to the world. Stay with this feeling for as long as possible.

Hydrate. Pour yourself a cup of tea and enjoy. Namaste.

Spill the Tea on Meditation

Beauty is not in the face; Beauty is a light in the heart.

Kahil Gibran

Tea & MEditation

Meditation is a form of relaxation. It is about finding a few minutes to breathe, look within, and listen to your body. You can practise mindful meditation by yourself or with others.

I like the phrase in Mark 18:20, *For where two or three are gathered together in my name, there am I in the midst of them.* I remember a yoga teacher saying that it is good to meditate in three's. It is also wise to meditate alone – simply retire to a room where you will not be disturbed or go outside and sit down where it is comfortable, relax, and focus on your breath. You can pull a scarf over your head or pull your hoodie up to help you to relax.

There will be days when you will want to be on your own to enjoy the silence or to enjoy the music and the atmosphere around you. There will also be days when you will want or need to find people in your tribe who will be silent with you. Today, find a place to relax and let go of whatever does not serve you. There are several ways to begin your meditation. Visualize or focus on a particular object (a candle, a gem stone), a mantra (*So Hum*), or 528Hz healing music.

Relax. Put your hands on your heart centre and connect with your heart energy. Feel your chest raise and lower with every breath. Ask that you be lifted up above any situation you are experiencing. Know that you are safe and protected. Visualize filling your body and mind with love. If it helps, silently chant the words *I love you* for a few moments.

Focus on your breath. Try to make your exhale longer than your inhale, e.g., breathe in for four, exhale for six. If this count is difficult, focus on a breathing pattern that is comfortable for you. Continue deep breathing until you feel relaxed. If you find that you are interrupted while in meditation, accept the situation, do what needs to be done, and then come back to your meditation time. You do not need to add on any extra time unless you feel it is necessary.

Be mindful. Relax your face and neck muscles. Relax your shoulders. Breathe into every cell in your body. Begin to focus your attention and awareness on your chosen object or mantra. Become aware of the present moment and know that each breath is a gift. When a negative thought or image arises, let it go, and return your focus to your breath. The past and the future exist only in your thoughts. Be committed to the moment. Rest in awareness and know you are safe. You are protected.

Rest in this safe space for as long as you need. When you are ready, gently move your toes and fingers. Shift and stretch your body. Your healing process is completed.

Hydrate. Choose your favourite tea, reflect on how your body is feeling, and enjoy your day. Namaste.

Never be in a hurry; do everything quietly and in a calm spirit. Do not lose your inner peace for anything whatsoever, even if your whole world seems upset.

St. Francis de Sales

My Musings

I enjoy a cup of chamomile tea. Chamomile tea helps me to relax, to calm my anxiety, as well as to help me think a little deeper. As I enjoy a hot cup of chamomile tea I sometimes become intrigued with the universe as a field of creative intelligence. The universe was created over 13.8 billion years ago or, perhaps it has always existed. Our solar system is approximately 4.6 billion years old. My understanding is that our knowledge of the universe comes from theoretical physics, direct observations by astronomers, and from evidence that is beyond my comprehension. I just know it exists. I exist. I am made of the same stuff as the stars. I wonder about the minds that study this science and those who travel in space if they believe in a higher power. As I drink my tea, I think about the infinite possibilities that had to occur so that life can exist on this planet. I also think about all the possibilities that may occur during the day and what actually will happen.

One day I was researching ways to help keep mosquitoes away. A group of friends were coming over to sit outside around the campfire, share stories, and roast marshmallows. An online article I read said to burn chamomile flowers. I had a few chamomile plants in the garden so I gathered them and placed the flowers into the campfire. I am not sure it worked to keep the mosquitoes away, but it was a great conversation starter. I did make a pot of chamomile tea and the campfire conversation was wonderful. There is a time to share and a time to listen. Listening helps one to grow just a little bit wiser.

Meditation with Chamomile

Our feelings arise from our thoughts. What you are thinking about is what you will bring into the current moment. I like the quote above from St. Francis de Sales. If we are not thinking negative thoughts, then we will not lose our inner peace. We will not block the positive and loving energy that will help us grow and heal. Positive thoughts help to create positive feelings. Our feelings and emotions are valid; however, negativity will block our ability to experience and manifest love, joy, and any positive emotions we desire.

We live in a world of thought. Many philosophers and spiritualists have been quoted to say that thought is not reality and yet our reality is created through thought. Each one of us lives through and sees our own perception of life and each one of us has a different perception and expectation of what life is about. Our stories are different. The labels we wear, the expectations, and our choice to take them on, whether it is mother, father, daughter, son, or another label, are not the same for everyone. We may cause suffering with thinking, not just negative thinking, but by comparing what we think is our reality to something that has been created by someone or something else. Our thoughts and beliefs help us to live in a world created by the expectations and perceptions of someone or something else. Is this world reflective of love?

Our perception is based on what we see, hear, feel, taste, smell, touch, and sense. Memory helps us understand the world we have created around us. Understanding a situation is not easy. Our truth and our reality is made up of our expectations, thoughts, beliefs, experiences, memories, fears, and perception. When a tree falls in the forest, do you hear it? Did you see it fall? Did you hear it crash, rustling the leaves and branches of other trees as it came down to rest on the ground or on another tree? What did you observe or perceive what actually happened? We can experience or visualize the event and come to realize that what we observed or imagined is different for everyone. It is just another way of looking at the situation. So when your world seems chaotic, make yourself a hot cup of chamomile tea, relax, and enjoy the moment.

Nature/Tea Focus
Chamomile

The name chamomile is generally thought to mean *earth apple* due to its floral taste and fragrance. The plant may not produce a lot of blooms. These edible flowers are thought to have healing properties that boost mental health and protect the skin. For centuries, chamomile has been used in food and for making teas and herbal medicines, as well as for its beauty in gardens.

The plant is noted to have many health benefits; however, one needs to be careful of herbs and possible allergies. Chamomile flowers have a symbolic meaning of rest, peace, poise, and calmness. The flower is also seen as a sign of renewal and rebirth due to its ability to bloom for long periods. The plant is strong. I love to see chamomile in gardens and to reflect on its properties.

Chamomile Oat Cookies

Cream together 2/3 cups (150 g) butter
2/3 cups (150 g) shortening
1 cup (220 g) brown sugar

Add:
3 cups (300 g) oatmeal
2 cups (240 g) all purpose flour
2 1/2 teaspoons chamomile (good quality from tea bags)
1/4 teaspoon salt
1/2 teaspoon baking soda

Work the dough until just mixed and crumbly. Add 1/4 to 1/3 cup water slowly as needed and keep mixing a few minutes more just until dough comes together in a solid mass, not too dry (crumbles from a spoon) but not too wet and sticky.

Scoop the dough by large tablespoons onto a cookie sheet. Press flat with fingers to 1/4 - 1/2 inch thick.

Bake at 350 - 375 degrees for 15 - 20 minutes until golden. Transfer to cooling rack.

Recipe makes about 40 small or 20 large oat cakes. To re-crisp, warm them in 200 degree oven on a cookie sheet for 5-10 minutes.

Chamomile Latte with Honey

This is a tea is made with chamomile tea, steamed milk, and honey.

Ingredients
1½ cups (375 ml) water
4 chamomile tea bags or
2-3 tablespoons (30-45 ml) loose leaves
1½ cups (375 ml) warm milk (your choice of "milk" beverage)
Add honey to taste
Ground cinnamon to sprinkle on top

Directions
You may want to preheat your teapot with hot water and discard when ready. Bring water to a boil and pour into a teapot. Add tea bags. Steep four to six minutes then remove tea bags. Add honey to taste. In a small saucepan, heat milk until just warm. Remove and whisk until frothy. Pour the tea and frothy milk into one or two cups. Add some froth to the top. Sprinkle with ground cinnamon.

Chamomile Tea

3 to 4 tablespoons (45-60 g) fresh chamomile flowers
1 small fresh sprig of mint
1 cup (250 ml) boiling water

Pour boiling water into a teapot and then add the chamomile flowers and mint.

Strain to remove the flowers. Pour into cups and enjoy.

The flowers will stay fresh in the fridge for a few days if you are not going to use them right away. Chamomile tea helps to promote relaxation and sleep. If you are using dried chamomile flowers, you may want to add a sweetener to taste.

The self work that you do in silence will echo throughout every part of your life.

Michell C. Clark

Journal

Meditation can be silent. But it can also take the form of dancing, singing, or simply vocalizing your prayers to God. Meditation is not defined by silence. It is defined by reflection.

Brandon Robbins

Journal

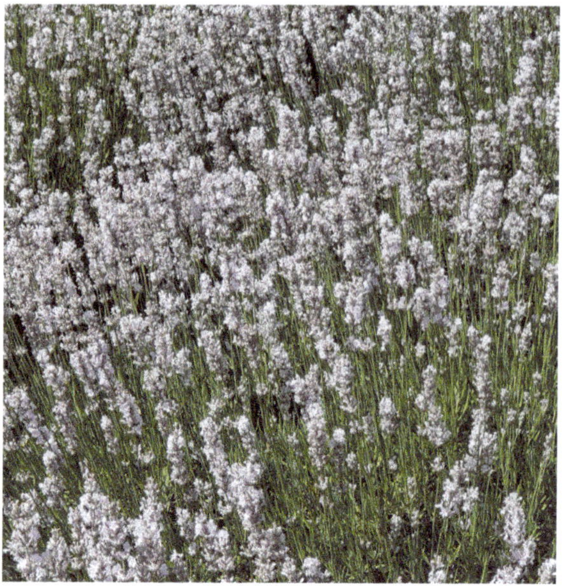

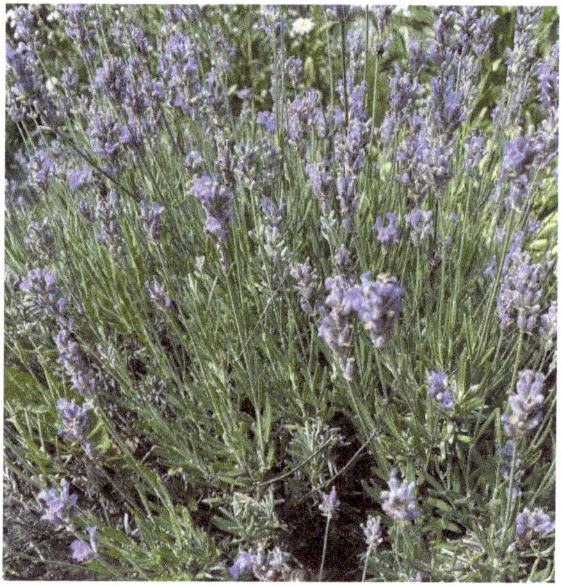

Meditation with Lavender

Poem

Journal Prompts & Self-Reflection Questions

Affirmations

Tea & MEditation

My Musings

Nature/Tea Focus—Lavender and Lavender-White Tea blend

Affirmations

Affirmations are short, powerful, positive statements. They are meant to encourage you to live a life filled with gratitude. An affirmation may motivate and inspire you. Repeating an affirmation daily, whether you speak it, write it, or think it, is a positive way to help shape your reality. It will help you to remain in the state of gratitude throughout the day. An example of an affirmation is, *I am not defined by how others see me, but by who I know I am.*

Being

like the trees and bushes Being
they need nourishment for without it they cannot live
existence is not the answer
they drink the water and minerals from mother earth
she nourishes them
without judgment
Being
even in the face of this new normality,
my life goes on and imparts a message
of healing
for myself and to the world.

Maureen Lowden

Journal Prompts & Self-Reflection Questions

(Use this space to journal and self-reflect)

> **What do I want? Where do I want to be? How does pressure or fear affect my life?** Everything is energy. Fear is a low vibration energy and it attracts low vibration energy to you. The same is true for the higher vibrations of love and joy. If you want or desire something become aware of your attachment to it. Eckhart Tolle said that, "*Attachment to things drops away when you no longer seek to find yourself in them.*" The questions and answers that we reflect upon help us to understand ourselves better. Questions are helpful for reflection about who we are in the present moment. A simple question can help us to explore a deeper insight into our lives. *Where do I want to be in two years? How will I get there?* There are no wrong answers. There are no wrong questions. There are powerful questions that will help lead us into reflection and inquiry about our authentic self. Explore questions that arise within you and write down your thoughts in your journal. When meditating, release any thoughts and answers that come to you and see where your journey takes you.

What season of life am I in right now?

___

How does this season affect my life?

___

What is special about this season?

Affirmations

Earth and Ground

Affirmation

_____
_____
_____
_____
_____
_____

Visualization

_____
_____
_____
_____
_____

Intention / Action Plan

_____
_____
_____
_____
_____
_____

I am worthy of what I desire.
I am Spirit.
I am self-confident.
I am protected.
I am guided and grounded.
I am a master receiver.
I will be fearless in all situations.
I deserve respect.
I am respectful to myself and others.
I am enough.
I am in charge of my life.
I am balanced in all areas of my life.
I am connected to everything and all that is.
I see every challenge as an opportunity for growth.
I know that no matter how long the night, the day is sure to come and the sun will rise.
My love will reach where it has never reached before.

We are all here for a purpose. Our greatest weakness lies in giving up. Our greatest glory lies in rising every time we fall.

Thomas Edison

Tea & MEditation

Find a place that is comfortable and that supports your back. If you are sitting down, place your feet firmly on the floor or the ground. Rest your hands comfortably on your lap. Begin your meditation by focusing on your breath. Inhale several deep breaths to a count of three and exhale fully to a count of six. Breathe so that you feel comfortable and relaxed. There is no rush. Allow your body to sink into the chair or sofa.

For a few minutes continue with a gentle breathing pattern. Inhale and exhale gently and with your mind slowly examine your whole body. While you are taking a breath in, focus on areas where you feel pain and energy blockages and on the exhale visualize any pain and soreness leaving your body. Continue to scan your body for any energy blockages and visualize the negative and stale energy leaving your body out through the bottom of your feet and through your hands.

Breathe in silently repeating the word *joy* and on the exhale silently say the word *peace*. Place your hands on your heart centre and sense a beautiful golden light all around you and within you. Visualize this healing, golden light filling your body and pushing negative energy and thoughts out of your body. When your thoughts are distracting you, continue to focus on the words *joy* while breathing in and *peace* while exhaling. Take your time. You are safe and protected.

When you are ready, release the words and rest in this healing light. You may want to return to the deep breathing pattern and inhale for three and exhale for six before returning to your normal breathing.

Wake up your body by moving your toes and fingers. Roll your shoulders and gently move your body. Return to a relaxed breathing pattern. Send love out to the world and hold all those you love in healing thoughts. Know that even though everything will change, you are in control of your emotions and feelings. Your treasure is within.

Hydrate. Pick up a pencil or pen and journal about your thoughts, feelings, and any healing you experienced. Pour yourself a cup of tea.

Namaste.

You must be the change you wish to see in the world.

Gandhi

Tea & MEditation

Get into a comfortable sitting position. The practice of pranayama involves breathing exercises. *Prana* means life energy and *yama* generally means breath control.

Bring your awareness within, take a few deep breaths in through both nostrils and exhale through your mouth slowly. You may wish to close your eyes when doing this breathing exercise. Using your thumb and index finger you will alternate your inhale and exhale through your nostrils.

When you are ready, place your thumb to close the right nostril and inhale through your left nostril. Pressing your index finger on the left nostril, exhale through the right nostril by releasing your thumb. Inhale through your right nostril, lift your index finger, place your thumb on your right nostril and exhale through the left. Inhale through the left, hold, lift your thumb, close the left nostril with your index finger and exhale through the right. Inhale right, hold, lift your index finger and exhale left nostril.

Move through this practice a few more times at your own pace, inhaling and exhaling with a rhythmic flow. Release your hand and return to normal breathing.

When you are ready, ground yourself. Place your feet firmly on the ground or floor and on the inhale silently say to yourself the words "I am" and on the exhale "grounded." You may wish to repeat this affirmation a few more times. Move your toes and fingers and gently wake up your body. Send love out to the world and hold all those you love in healing thoughts.

Hydrate. Pour yourself a cup of tea.

Namaste.

Service to others is the rent you pay for your room here on earth.

Muhammad Ali

My Musings

My aunt and grandmother loved the smell of lavender. One Christmas, my grandmother asked me to buy English lavender perfume and bath salts for my aunt. I love shopping and accepted the task. The season of Christmas is wonderful. People are smiling and chatting. Carollers are singing and walking the malls. The decorations are beautiful. I got distracted by the season and set off to find a gift. There were so many options and other choices I thought my aunt would enjoy. I remember thinking she still had some bath salts so instead of buying the lavender gift, I thought I would surprise my aunt and buy her a winter tam. The hat was adorable and I knew it would look great on her. However, when my aunt opened her gift from my grandmother (her mother), she looked confused, my grandmother looked confused, and I was disappointed when I did not see any smiles. I was helping my grandmother with her Christmas shopping but I got caught up in my own ideas and thoughts. Every situation has a lesson. The lesson I learned was that service or helping others is not always what you think others want, might like, or even need. You need to carefully listen to their story to understand better. Service is not always being concerned about yourself and your choices. You need to listen carefully to others as well as to your inner voice.

When you ask yourself questions that are meaningful to you such as *Who am I? What do I desire? What are my next steps?* take the time to listen to the answers and then set your intention. My wish throughout my journey is to not be alone. My social and emotional connections help me create a more purposeful and meaningful life. I enjoy volunteering and I have friends, family, and community. If the relationship however is not meaningful and purposeful then I tend to seek out my own company. I am content being on my own and the older I get the more I feel free to be myself. I do not connect solitude with loneliness. I am on a path that I helped create with my Higher Power in a world that, I believe, does not see its potential. We are blinded by the illusion of materialism, the expectations and perceptions of our thoughts and beliefs, and the stories and culture of our ancestors. We are busy looking at, comparing, and thinking about our differences and doing and trying to understand in the busyness of the world around us.

Relationships can be difficult to maintain as they take time to develop, require trust and understanding, honesty, respect, patience, and personal interaction. I know that all things are possible with the Divine's help when I ask from a place of compassion, empathy, and spirit. *Ask and it will be given to you, seek and you will find, knock and the door shall be opened to you* (Luke 11:9). Out of the billions of years and the vastness of the universe, we are here for such a short time to learn our purpose. We can work together in a co-creative process consciously or unconsciously. We can move through life aware or unaware. The design of your life is a choice.

Do I listen? Do I understand? Messages from the Divine Source can be heard if we listen, if we turn off our cell phones, if we listen in silence, if we use our eyes to see what is really going on and trust our instincts. I wish I could say I learned my lesson from the Christmas shopping task but the opportunity to listen has come up quite a few times in my life. Did I listen to my inner voice? Did I listen to others? Relationships, with yourself and others, need to be tended to just like the lavender plant grown for its fragrance. The plant needs a specific environment to grow beautiful and strong. It reaches into the ground to find nutrients and water to live. Relationships need to be nurtured in the right environment and given just the right amount of attention to become beautiful and strong. When I meditate and focus on mindfulness, I ask for those values that will help me grow strong in spirit, body, and mind.

If the lesson is not learned and understood, it will keep coming back into your life until it is learned and understood. I have stayed in relationships or life experiences for perhaps too long. Perhaps you have too? I would question if what I was thinking or feeling was my intuition, my inner voice, or was it fear. Did I stay in a relationship too long because of fear? There are no wrong questions ... just questions. There are no wrong answers ... just choices. Choices of spirit are always resonating in the highest energy level. That high energy level is brought out of love.

Your journey and my journey, whether we are ready or not, will change. Did I plant my hopes in fertile soil? Did I let my roots branch out to find nourishment? Will my questions be answered? *Galatians 5:22-23* refers to the fruits of the Spirit as love, joy, peace, patience, kindness, goodness, faithfulness, gentleness, and self-control. Can I or others see these qualities in me? Do I desire these qualities? Have I asked to receive these gifts? Relationships go through many stages and listening to my inner voice is important at every stage. Did I listen every time the path changed? The path to abundance is perhaps listening to my soul and my inner voice.

Nature/Tea Focus
Lavender Tea and a White-Lavender Tea Blend

Lavender comes from the Latin word *lavare* — to wash. Lavender has a long history dating back to ancient Egypt and the Old World. I visited a lavender grower and explored their lavender fields. Lavender, a native plant of western Mediterranean regions, is now grown in many countries. There are many varieties of lavender, including white lavender and several shades of purple. English lavender is one of the more popular types of lavender used in cooking and is known for its medicinal properties such as anti-inflammatory, antibacterial, and antifungal properties. The French lavender is generally used for oils as it produces more buds. Lavender is also used in products to help treat acne, eczema, stress, and headaches.

Lavender tea normally has a strong, aromatic, perfume smell. Blending lavender with other herbs provides a refreshing drink. The qualities of lavender make a calming and relaxing tea. It is important to use organic lavender or lavender that is for culinary purposes. Only non-faded, deep-blue flowers should be used. The flowers will turn the tea a purplish-blue colour.

Lavender Tea

For one cup (250 ml) of lavender tea, you will need approximately 1 to 1½ teaspoons (5 to 7 ml) of dried lavender buds and boiling water. Let the lavender buds steep for 2 to 4 minutes and serve with honey and a slice of lemon. The longer you let the lavender steep, the stronger the taste.

Lavender-White Tea Blend

To make a lavender-white tea blend, brew a blend of lavender buds, white tea leaves, and chamomile flowers. You will need approximately 1 teaspoon (5 ml) of the blend. Brew for about 2 to 4 minutes or to your preference.

White teas are a specialty tea and the production of white tea is spreading around the world. White tea is known for its delicate taste, aroma, and is less likely to contain caffeine. The harvest lasts for approximately two weeks in the spring. Only the delicate whole buds and whole leaves are preserved during the production process. White teas were, at one time, reserved only for emperors and other high-ranking officials.

Lavender Cookies

Ingredients:

½ cup butter and ½ cup shortening or 1 cup (227 g) butter softened
1 1/4 cups (250 g) sugar
2 large eggs
1 teaspoon (5 ml) vanilla extract
2 1/4 cups (280 g) all-purpose flour
3 1/2 teaspoons (17 ml) culinary dried lavender flowers
1 teaspoon (5 ml) baking powder
1/2 teaspoon (2.5 ml) salt

Directions:

Meditation with Lavender

1. Preheat oven to 375°F (190°C).
2. Cream butter, shortening, and sugar together until light and fluffy.
3. Add eggs, one at a time, beating well after each addition.
4. Add vanilla extract.
5. In a separate bowl, whisk flour, lavender, baking powder, and salt and mix until completely combined.
6. Gradually beat the dry ingredients into the creamed mixture. The dough should be soft and easy to handle.
7. Drop by rounded teaspoonfuls 1 inch (2 cm) apart onto lightly greased baking sheet or covered with parchment paper.
8. Bake until golden brown, approximately 8 to 10 minutes or until cookies are slightly browned around the edges. Cool 2 minutes before removing to wire racks. Store in an airtight container.

Note: Metric measurements may be slightly different.

Spill the Tea on Meditation

You are not just here to work, pay the bills, and relax for a few weeks out of the year. You are a compendium of virtues that are waiting to be activated. Discover them and put them to good use.

Tomás Navarro

Journal

Meditation with Lavender

Surround yourself only with people who are going to lift you higher.

Oprah Winfrey

Journal

Spill the Tea on Meditation

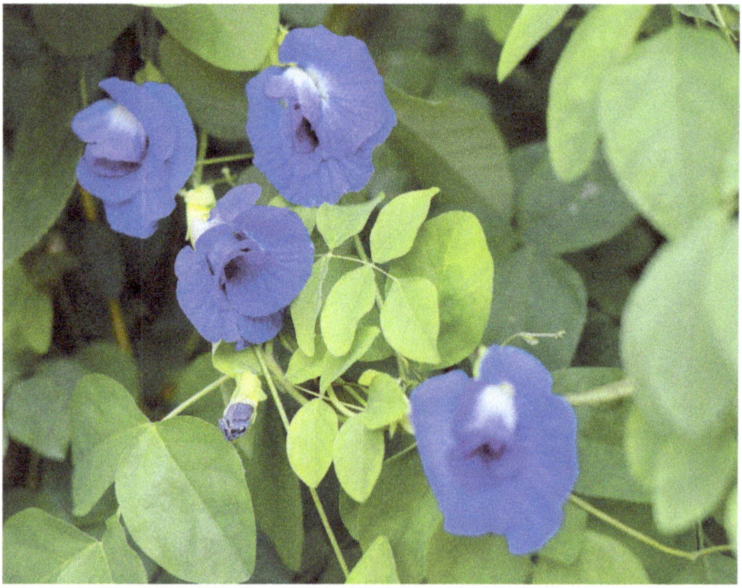

Meditation with Butterfly-Pea Flower

Journal Prompts & Self-Reflection Questions

Affirmations

Tea & MEditation

My Musings

Nature/Tea Focus—Butterfly-Pea Tea

Intentions – What is your deepest desire?

An intention is a starting point that

- ✓ You set for yourself
- ✓ Identifies your desires
- ✓ Is clear
- ✓ Shifts any limiting beliefs
- ✓ Shifts your perspective to empowering and positive thoughts
- ✓ Helps you to detach from the outcome, to surrender, and let go
- ✓ Helps you to release control of your expectations

When you reflect and look inside yourself and understand your deepest desire then your desire is your intention. Your intention becomes your will and bringing your will into consciousness becomes your deed. *Your deed helps to shape your destiny.*

Spill the Tea on Meditation

Meditation with Butterfly-Pea Flower

Embrace Life

Walk gently
fear, jealousy, anger, impatience
rise above the hidden traps surrounding you
Walk gently

Breathe softly
compassion, understanding, sun, moon
rise above the judgment, the criticism
Breathe softly

Embrace lightly
strength, courage, forgiveness, wonderment
rise above the real and imagined traps
Embrace lightly

Walk gently
away from the aloneness
away from the imagined
embrace the struggle

Breathe softly
rise above with grace and gratitude
for the gift of life

Embrace lightly for
you are not alone

Maureen Lowden

Journal Prompts & Self-Reflection Questions

(Use this space to journal and self-reflect)

> *What am I grateful for?* We can be grateful for many different experiences, from taking our first breath to having a cup of tea. When we are born our first breath is an inhale. We breathe *prana*, a life-giving force, a universal energy that flows around us, in and through our body and is in everything. We are grateful for our stories, feeling compassion and empathy for others, for being able to enjoy nature, and even for the trials and the darkness that we encounter as these experiences help us to learn. When we are grateful for our truth, we do not have to say anything. Answering the question *What am I grateful for?* is a way to say thank you to a power greater than ourselves. It is a time of self-reflection.

What does being grateful mean to you?

_____

_____

_____

_____

_____

_____

_____

Meditation with Butterfly-Pea Flower

Will you let "gratefulness" transform you?

_____

_____

_____

_____

_____

What relationships are you grateful for?

_____

_____

_____

_____

_____

What blessings are you grateful for and why?

_____

_____

_____

_____

_____

_____

Affirmations

Harmony and Resolution

Affirmation	
_____	I am my light.
_____	I have the power to create change.
_____	I am resilient and strong.
_____	I am comforted and harmony is restored
_____	I receive change with an open mind.
_____	My power is unlimited.
_____	I am at peace with myself.
Visualization	The Universe is always working in my favour.
_____	There is always another way to bring about positive change and make it happen.
_____	I am secure and safe being who I am.
_____	I am a great communicator.
_____	I am blessed.
_____	I am a valuable human being.
Intention / Action Plan	Today is the best day of my life.
_____	Thank you for this beautiful life.
_____	Every breath I take fills me with peace.
_____	
_____	
_____	
_____	

Meditation with Butterfly-Pea Flower

Darkness cannot drive out darkness; only light can do that.
Hate cannot drive out hate; only love can do that.

Martin Luther King, Jr.

Tea & MEditation

Begin by finding a comfortable place to sit or lie down. Rest your hands in your lap. If it is comfortable, gently bring together (on each hand) the tips of your thumb and index finger and holding your other three fingers straight. This hand posture is the *Gyan mudra* and it is used to help with concentration and when seeking knowledge.

Focus on your breath allowing it to connect you to the present moment. Visualize a pillar of light moving through you, grounding you to the earth, and spreading its rays like the roots of a tree when it touches earth. Imagine the pillar of light spreading out all around you and then visualize the light travelling back up through your feet, flowing up your spine to the crown chakra, and up to the heavens. You are safe. All is well. The light is clearing all negativity from your space. It is time to release your fears and anxiety.

Relax and be at peace as you are firmly grounded. Silently repeat the mantra *Shanti or Peace*. When your thoughts distract you, gently return to the mantra. Breathe in the mantra *Shanti*, hold for four, breathe out *Shanti*, hold for four. Meditate on peace.

When you are ready say these affirmations:

I am peaceful.
You are peaceful.
We are all peaceful.

You may want to repeat the mantra three times or more. Do what is comfortable. When it is time, gently move your toes and your fingers. Shift your body and feel yourself wakening to the sounds around you. Send loving thoughts out to the world leaving no one out. Know you are enough.

Pour yourself a cup of tea. Keep the teapot close so you can refill your cup.

Namaste.

Meditation with Butterfly-Pea Flower

Love the Lord God with your whole heart, your whole soul, and your whole mind; and love your neighbour as yourself.

Matthew 22:37-40

Tea & MEditation

Begin by going to a safe place where you are comfortable and relaxed. It may be best to be seated for this meditation but you can be anywhere where you feel peaceful. Start by taking in three deep breaths and visualize a pink veil of energy surrounding you. Feel your breath going deeper with each breath. Breathe in the pink energy creating a presence of love and peace around and within you. Breathe out anything that does not serve you. Release any stress and tension. Release the fear of the future and let go of the past.

Return to a normal breathing pattern, expand this loving pink energy within your heart centre, and feel the energy surrounding you and keeping you safe. Stay with this feeling until you are ready to move this energy throughout your body. When you are ready, send the pink energy from your heart centre to your organs, to the front and back solar plexus chakra, to your root chakra, down through your legs and out through your feet to Mother Earth. Send this peaceful loving energy deep into the earth acknowledging the earth's bounty and beauty. Send this pink energy to everyone and everything in the universe. Send this loving energy to friends, family, to your community, to your neighbours, and to those with whom you have experienced conflict. Let go of any thoughts that come to you.

When you are ready, place your hands on your heart chakra and open your heart chakra to receive the energy from Mother Earth. Bring the energy back to yourself and acknowledge your gifts and your beauty. You are love. You are loved. As you visualize the energy returning to your heart chakra, imagine you are being filled with pink and white crystalline energy. Rest here until you are ready to move this crystalline energy up to your throat chakra, visualize moving it to your third eye chakra, and to your crown chakra.

The white crystalline energy surrounds you. You are receiving this beautiful crystalline energy and releasing anything that does not serve you. Visualize the white energy as it brings you to a place of relaxation and peace.

Acknowledge the goodness within your heart centre as well as the pain inherent in blessings. Silently chant the mantra, *Shanti* or the word *Peace*. Become aware of the silence between the chants.

Rest in this energy for as long as you wish. When you are ready, become aware of your breath and begin to notice your breathing pattern. Move your fingers, hands, and toes. Gently move your body.

As you continue with your day, know you have a voice and in all relationships and connections you continue to communicate with thoughtfulness and love.

Hydrate. Pour yourself a cup of tea. Namaste.

Meditation with Butterfly-Pea Flower

Anyone who thinks that they are too small to make a difference has never tried to fall asleep with a mosquito in the room.

Christine Todd Whitman

My Musings

When you make a cup of tea with the Butterfly-Pea flower, its properties turn the water blue and if you add a little bit of lemon, the tea will turn pink or purple. Magic!

A baby is born and you see how beautiful life can be with this tiny individual. The transformation of life from tiny cells into a human being is a miracle. My vision when I had a child was to be protective and to believe in miracles. My baby was wrapped in pink.

Through the wonderful world of science, I saw my first grandchild before he was born. He was wrapped in blue. I now have three grandchildren and each one is a precious miracle.

Another miracle. Another transformation.

Blue is often a part of a western culture wedding tradition. According to an old English rhyme, the bride wears *Something Olde, Something New, Something Borrowed, Something Blue, A Sixpence in your Shoe* to bless the couple on their journey together.

When we look up into the sky, our eyes may see blue, grey, pink, white, yellow and other colours. The colours merge together to create something beautiful. We may see clouds of many different shapes and colours. I can often name some clouds as I have seen elephants, a racing horse, angels, faces, fingers reaching for me, and even Mickey Mouse.

The colours in the rainbow are remembered with the acronym *ROY G BIV.* That is how I learned and taught the colours to my Kindergarten class - red, orange, yellow, green, blue, indigo, violet. The colours of the chakra centres – our energy centres. When you are meditating imagine these colours being poured over you and creating the life you imagine where there is no suffering. Imagine!

When you look at a rainbow, do you see all the colours? Do you see how the colours blend together? Sometimes a colour seems to be missing but my faith tells me it is there. Perhaps it is already dissipating so I trust that all the colours of the rainbow appeared. There does not seem to be one colour vying for recognition at the expense of the others. I just see the magic of crystals and the beauty of colour. I give thanks for my sight and for my imagination.

Our chakra energy centres flow and connect with one another. Our energy centres are a rainbow of colours within representing inclusivity and diversity, love and friendship. There is no separation – not from each other, not from our Higher Power, and not from anything that is. Everything is connected.

When I taught Kindergarten, the children were excited to see red and blue become purple, and red and yellow become orange. I wonder why we are so accepting of all colours yet when we see colours and differences in human beings we are not so accepting. What makes one colour better than another? If we are looking at everything through the eyes of our spirit, there would be no differences. Everything is just as it should be.

Stay curious. Stay open. Be aware. Be willing to bend a little. Enjoy the miraculous results of life.

Nature/Tea Focus

The butterfly-pea flower is commonly known by several names depending upon where it is grown. Two other names, that I know of, for the butterfly-pea flower, is blue pea or pigeonwings. For centuries, the butterfly-pea flower has been known for the deep blue colour of the petals. The flowers are used for their supposed medicinal properties and the beverage or tea is usually served with lemon and honey. Adding lemon juice to the tea changes the pH balance of the drink, making it change colour from a deep blue to purple.

Butterfly-Pea Flower Tea

Butterfly-pea tea can be made by pouring boiling water into a tea pot and then gently add the butterfly-pea flower. The taste is light and aromatic; however, if your preference is to have a sweet tea, then add a little honey. Some people choose to add a slice of lemon or a dash of lemon juice to give it an additional boost.

To make Blue tea, combine Oolong tea, butterfly-pea flower, and calendula petals in a tea bag. Pour boiling water into the tea pot and gently add the tea bag filled with the tea blend.

Meditation with Butterfly-Pea Flower

*Never go in search of love, go in search of life,
and life will find you the love you seek.*

Atticus

Journal

_____
_____
_____
_____
_____
_____
_____
_____
_____
_____
_____
_____
_____
_____
_____
_____

Spill the Tea on Meditation

Peace is the result of retraining your mind to process life as it is, rather than how you think it should be.

Wayne Dyer

Journal

Meditation with Butterfly-Pea Flower

Meditation with Matcha and Green Tea

Journal Prompts & Self-Reflection Questions

Affirmations

Tea & MEditation

My Musings

Nature/Tea Focus - Matcha and Green Tea

Mudras (The power in our hands)

A *mudra* is a symbolic gesture that is performed with the hands and fingers and stimulates areas of the body and helps energy flow through and in your body.

To perform a *mudra*, the pressure of the fingers should be very light and fine, and your hands should be relaxed. The flexibility of the hands has a direct relationship to the flexibility of the entire body. If our bodies are tense, this tension will be expressed at a corresponding area on the hands. A simple *mudra* is the *anjali mudra* – two hands, palms facing each other, in a welcome greeting. Bringing the hands together at your heart centre is generally accepted as meaning, *I honour the divinity in you.*

Staying Power

Patience, Wait
Be the Witness
Earth keeps giving
Water and land working together
hot molten lava cooling so
life exists
Universe keeps giving
expanding
burning brilliant stars
energy exists
Patience, Wait
reflect on the fire within
creating a new form
from the ashes
billions of years to create
You
Patience, Wait
Be the Witness
in a moment of time

Maureen Lowden

Journal Prompts & Self-Reflection Questions

(Use this space to journal and self-reflect)

> ***What is my purpose in life?*** Your true purpose connects you to your higher self. It is your unique vibration that informs everything you do and everything you are. Your purpose transcends your physical form and is the reason why you get up in the morning. Your purpose is not about a specific goal to achieve; it informs your goals. It is the very nature of your being and why you are here on earth. Your purpose and intention influences your behaviour. You have within an inner wisdom that governs or guides you. It is an intuitive wisdom and you can distinguish this wisdom from the many voices you hear. Once we become aware of our true purpose, we can step into our full potential.

How do I feel about my workplace or home?

_____

_____

_____

_____

_____

_____

_____

Does my family or my workplace support me?

___

Am I respected? Do I know my boundaries?

___

Do I feel confident in what I have chosen to do?

___

Affirmations

Strength and Guidance

Affirmation

_____
_____
_____
_____
_____

Visualization

_____
_____
_____
_____
_____

Intention / Action Plan

_____
_____
_____
_____
_____

My life is constantly being made new.
I am not damaged, broke, or abandoned. I am whole and loved.
I am healing.
I am rediscovering myself.
I am starting a new day and embracing my journey.
There is grace in trust and peace in release.
I am meant to be where I am.
I am in the right place and at the right time.
I am experiencing life in new ways so that I will grow toward love, forgiveness, and peace.
I honour my pain and grow in strength.
I have confidence and make choices that support my desires.
I am peaceful.
I am resiliant.
I am releasing energy that I no longer need to hold on to.
I am grounded in the present.

Since God is, He is to be found in the questions as well as the answers.

Elie Wiesel, Open Heart

Tea & MEditation

Find a place where you can feel or see nature—e.g., a tree, plants in your home, a river or lake, etc. Take three deep breaths. Use the four-two-six-two count. Breathe in for a count of four through your nose, hold for a count of two, and exhale for a count of six though your mouth. Feel your chest rising and falling with each breath. When you are ready, let the count go and return to your natural breathing pattern.

Any thoughts that come to you, recognize them as part of the collective energy field, they are not your own. You are not your thoughts. Let them go. Divine guidance is loving and supportive.

Close your eyes and rest for a few minutes. Relax your body and release any tension. Receive the healing and the gifts that are being given to you. You are a master receiver and give thanks. You are grateful.

When you are ready, open your eyes and gently move your body. Pour yourself a cup of tea. Receive your healing gifts and let them sink into your conscious thoughts. Feeling relaxed and thoughtful breathe your gifts in and breathe them out. When you are ready take your gifts out to the world. A smile, a simple nod of your head, or saying hello is all it takes to heal and forgive. And so it is.

Your healing is complete. Namaste.

*When the power of love overcomes the love of power,
the world will know peace.*

Jimi Hendrix

Tea & MEditation

Sometimes the body is ready to let go while the mind is still holding on. At other times, the mind may need to be patient while the body is processing an experience. Healing will come; be patient.

Find a comfortable place to sit or lie down. If you would like, light a candle or hold a healing crystal in your hand. You may want to close your eyes or look at the candle or crystal. If you are holding a crystal, try to feel the vibrations of the crystal.

It is time to clear the area around you of any negative energy. Imagine a white paper bag on the floor beside you. Do not pick up the bag. Put any negative thoughts, situations, or things you have to do into the bag, close it, and leave it there on the floor. There is nothing in the imagined bag that needs to be done immediately and you might not want to pick the bag up again. You are free to make this decision when you are ready.

Imagine you are completely surrounded by a glowing, golden light. You are safe. Breathe in and out slowly. In your heart centre there is a small golden light within you. Focus on your heart centre and allow the light to expand within you.

The light flows from your heart centre to your feet and from your heart centre to your crown. It fills every cell of your body. Say to yourself and repeat at least ten times, *I am love*. Feel it. Believe it. Stay in this light-healing visualization for as long as it feels good. When you are ready, ground yourself to the earth, and gently move your body.

You may want to pick up the bag with your wants or needs in it or visualize crumpling it up and sending it off to the clouds. Be patient with yourself. Bring your hands together at your heart centre in the *Anjali mudra*, send unconditional love out to the world, leaving out no one, and give thanks.

Pour yourself a cup of tea and enjoy your day. Namaste.

Anjali mudra

Meditation with Matcha and Green Tea

Green is the prime colour of the world, and that from which its loveliness arises.

Pedro Calderon de la Barca

My Musings

Do you remember your very first cup of green tea? Maybe you have never tasted the aromatic green tea before. Over the years green tea has become a go-to drink. It is known to have some health benefits. Green tea may help to increase your metabolism. Drinking a cup of green tea before bed time may help your body to burn calories while sleeping.

Green is the colour of the heart chakra. The heart chakra is located in the central channel of the spine near the physical heart. It is the fourth primary chakra.

The Sanskrit word for the heart chakra is *Anahata* which generally means *unstuck or unhurt*. When the heart chakra is open we become aware of the contradictory and duality of experiences, of love, and of past hurts. We become open to the possibility that two opposite forces can be integrated allowing for cooperation, collaboration, and a new world and personal perspective. The two opposite forces can build the bridge between them to allow the flow of understanding and recognition to move. I see. I hear. I understand. I forgive. I am sorry.

A peacemaker is someone who takes the initiative to get involved in conflicts with the intention of building bridges between people who hold different and seemingly contradictory experiences. Everyone has their own truth and their own perspective. This is true. Everyone needs to be at the table to resolve issues including the Divine for our ego alone will not be able to find the bridge of peace. We need to honour our boundaries, our efforts, and our true self.

I like this quote, *Sometimes we suffer in life, not because you were bad. But because you did not realize where and when to stop being good.* (Author unknown). We are born into a dual world and we search to find the balance in every experience, in every emotion, and every feeling.

A peacemaker honours and respects others, shares with those in need, is happy for those rejoicing, and prayerful with those mourning. When our heart chakra is open we want to be in-service to others and make every effort to live in peace. Peace is attainable.

Blessed are the peacemakers.

Nature/Tea Focus Matcha and Green Tea

Matcha tea and green tea leaves come from the same plant, the camelia sinensis . Matcha tea is traditionally used for the Japanese tea ceremony. Today, different matcha teas are combined to help balance their strengths and weaknesses.

The methods used to make matcha tea and green tea result in a much higher concentration of chlorophyll, polyphenols, and antioxidants than other tea types.

Matcha tea is the whole green leaf finely ground to a powered form. It is dissolved in water at a temperature of 75°C or 167°F, and whisked to create a frothy, nourishing beverage rich in vitamin C and antioxidants. The finest grades are sweet with no hint of bitterness. A quarter teaspoon of matcha tea is usually all that is needed although some methods provide instruction to use one rounded teaspoon.

Matcha tea is known for its health benefits. It can help to increase your energy levels. The long lasting effects can be attributed to L theanine and the polyphenols natural compounds slowing the release of caffeine into the body. Matcha tea may help to boost your immune system, stimulate metabolism, detoxify, boost concentration, and lower cholesterol levels.

Try adding matcha tea to your smoothie in the morning for that boost of energy. You might want to replace your coffee and energy drinks with matcha. You can mix it, shake it, blend it, or just enjoy it on its own.

Green tea is an unoxidized tea. The leaves are plucked, slightly withered, and then immediately cooked to preserve the green quality and prevent oxidization. The leaves are generally harvested three times a year with the first flush producing the highest quality leaves. The heating process differs greatly depending on the region and the tea maker's skilfulness and techniques.

Green tea is usually in leaf form and steeped in a bag or loose in a teapot or teacup. As with all teas, there is an optimal temperature for green tea. Pour the hot water into your teapot and then add the tea leaves. Let the fragrance rise. Do not pour boiling water over the leaves as this may slow the rise of the delicate aroma. Allow the tea to steep for approximately three minutes. Pour and strain. Add in your choice of sweetener.

Meditation with Matcha and Green Tea

You'll never change your life until you change something you do daily. The secret of your success is found in your daily routine.

John C. Maxwell

Journal

_____
_____
_____
_____
_____
_____
_____
_____
_____
_____
_____
_____
_____
_____
_____
_____
_____

Spill the Tea on Meditation

*My truth is not your truth. Your truth is not my truth.
Meditation helps me to heal and eases my sadness.
I accept my feelings and allow them to transform.*

M. Lowden

Journal

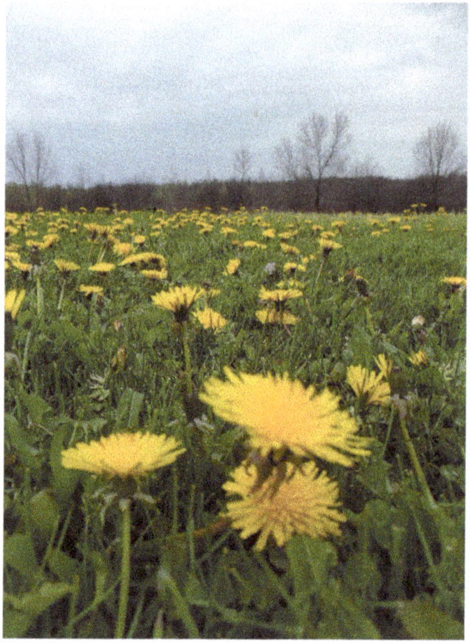

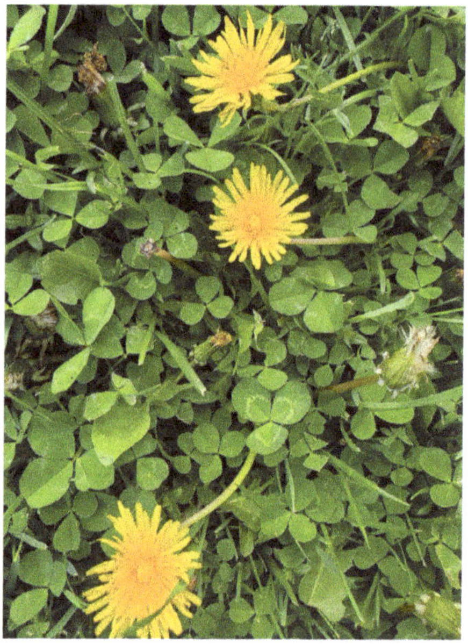

Meditation with Dandelions and Pineapples

Journal Prompts & Self-Reflection Questions

Affirmations

Tea & MEditation

My Musings

Nature/Tea Focus—Dandelion Tea and Pineapple Tea

Soul Searching Questions

What do I feel most passionate about?
What is the one thing I have always wanted to do?
What am I grateful for?
What would my ideal day look like?
What is holding me back?
What is my personal truth?
Who am I?

When you ask yourself a few soul searching questions, what responses pop up for you? There are no right or wrong answers. Your responses are thoughts. These thoughts may have little or no meaning or they might be profoundly significant for you. Ask a soul searching question before your meditation and if there are any answers, acknowledge the thoughts, then let them go and focus on your breathing.

Truth

truth doesn't stop
nor does it sleep
it remains ever present
even when you think it is hidden.
where am I?
here.
the present is
this moment.
now.
Connecting
with my true self.
Yet
I bring the past
into the present
reflecting.
tomorrow has yet to come.
Tomorrow brings gifts
from the past
and the present.
I should live in the present
The truth is always revealed
It cannot be hidden.

Maureen Lowden

Journal Prompts & Self-Reflection Questions

(Use this space to journal and self-reflect)

> What is my purpose? What do I really want to do in this life? What am I passionate about? When we are setting intentions we are called to discover our purpose and to explore our gifts. What fills you with a true sense of purpose? Have the courage to explore the questions and to be curious. We are called to co-create with our Creator, to be in this world and to be not of this world. We are invited to find meaning in our past and to learn from our life situations. We are asked to forgive; not forget, but to understand and find the guidance and resources to bring about positive change. Every one of us is on a different journey to connect to our authentic and true self. It is a daunting task but one in which you will be supported, guided, and loved toward your highest truth.

What would my life look like if I could do anything?

_____

_____

_____

_____

_____

_____

_____

What would my life look like if I gave myself permission to do what I really want to do?

_____

_____

_____

_____

_____

_____

_____

Is fear holding me back from what I really desire?

_____

_____

_____

_____

_____

_____

_____

_____

Affirmations

Ask and Receive, Knock and the door will be opened

Affirmation
_____
_____
_____
_____

Visualization
_____
_____
_____

Intention / Action Plan
_____
_____
_____
_____

I attract love and abundance.
I am grateful.
I appreciate all the ways I am unique.
I am successful.
I am made with divine intention.
I release everyone who, and everything that does not create joy in my life.
I am worthy.
I am adaptable.
I am flexible.
I welcome change with an open mind.
I open myself up to receive higher guidance.
I am open to limitless possibilities.
I believe in myself.

*Not everything that is faced can be changed;
but nothing can be changed until it is faced.*

James Baldwin

Tea & MEditation

In this meditation, we will begin by clearing your area of any negativity. Sit comfortably, focusing on your breath. Close your eyes and imagine the floor or the ground beneath you is covered in a white sheet. As you imagine this, gently take a few deep breaths and let the sheet move slowly up over your body.

Allow the sheet to rise up over your knees, then to your waist and then gently raise the sheet over your head. Once it is over your head, send the sheet up to the clouds.

Visualize the area below the sheet is now a rainbow of colours rising up. The rainbow of colours surrounds you. You feel safe and protected. Stay with this feeling as long as you wish.

With your eyes closed and your body relaxed, with both hands gently bend your ring finger and place it against the base of your thumb. Bring your thumb over your ring finger touching the knuckle. Keep your other fingers straight and relaxed. Bring your hands to your knees with the palms facing up and relax. The Surya* mudra increases the fire element or energy in the body. This mudra brings together the elements of fire and earth, activates a feeling of balance, and brings you into a positive state of Being.

When you are ready, gently move your body and take a few deep breaths. Stay with your healing energy and send love and healing energy out to the world, to your community, to family, and to friends.

Pour yourself a cup of tea and enjoy! Namaste.

*Surya in Sanskrit means *sun*. This mudra strengthens the solar / fire energy in the body. Practising the Surya mudra in the early morning hours opens you to benefit from the sun's energy. The mudra may also help to improve digestion and ward off colds.

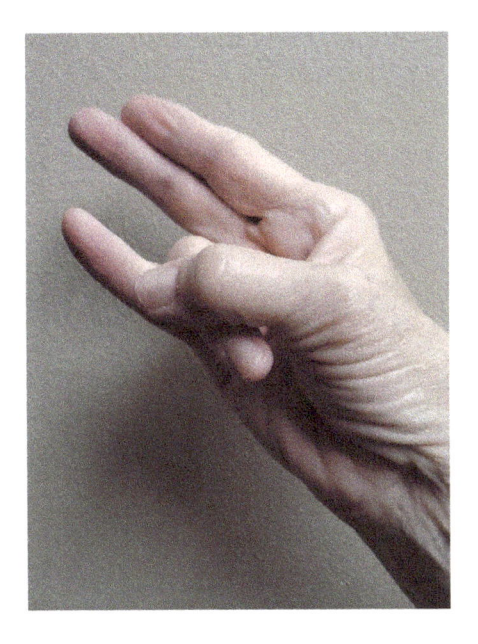

*Love is patient, love is kind. It does not envy,
it does not boast, it is not proud.*

1 Corinthians 13

Tea & MEditation

Find yourself a comfortable, quiet place where you will not be disturbed. Begin your meditation with gratefulness. You are grateful for this moment and for the breath of life. Breathe deeply for a few moments. Slowly count backwards from ten and then visualize yourself surrounded by a white light. Visualize a green light emanating from within your heart chakra and gradually uniting with the white light surrounding you. You are grateful for this moment and for life.

Continue breathing deeply and stay with this feeling for a few moments. Your heart is filled with the green light. Begin to move the light throughout your body. Send healing thoughts of love to every cell in your body. Any area where you feel pain, ask for healing. In any situation where you are experiencing difficulty, acknowledge it, and ask for healing. Continue breathing deeply for a few moments.

When you are ready, if possible, lengthen your exhale. Breathe in for a count of four and breathe out for a count of eight. Feel your chest expanding with the inhale and your lungs releasing the breath. Feel your shoulders relaxing. Continue this pattern until you feel you need to return to a normal breathing pattern.

When you have returned to a relaxed breathing pattern, ask yourself a soul searching question. *Who am I? What is my deepest desire? What difference can I make? What are my next steps?* Release any thoughts that come to you. For the next few minutes, quietly say to yourself the mantra *Shanti* or *Peace*. When you are ready, release the mantra, and rest in this peaceful state for as long as you wish.

Complete your meditation with a spiritual soul intention. Something that deeply resonates with you. Ask for guidance and listen for the answers. Let go of the how and focus on the what and why. Remain in silence for a few moments and focus on your breathing.

Slowly move your body, hands, fingers, toes, and feet. Awaken your body. Send loving thoughts out to the world and to all those who are in need.

Hydrate. Enjoy a cup of tea and relax. Namaste.

Every piece of the universe, even the tiniest little snow crystal, matters somehow. I have a place in the pattern, and so do you.

T.A. Barron

My Musings

My family shares stories. They are true stories, as far as we know, but everyone has their own perspective of them. Everyone has their own truth and everyone sees, hears, and feels events in one's life through their own perspective.

Dandelions have special memories for me. As a child, I remember picking them and then putting the yellow flower under a friend's chin to see if they liked butter. The yellow flowers turned my fingers yellow. When I picked the dandelion on a sunny day, the bright yellow flower would be fully opened to receive the warm sun's rays. I also remember making a ring from the stems of the dandelions and would wear the ring for as long as it held together.

Dandelions are strong. They can grow anywhere—in sidewalks, in cracks, in roads. They grow even where they are not wanted or appreciated. A friend shared a story about dandelions. She calls the seeds *wishes*, as they blow in the wind to find a place to grow and transform. It is a beautiful plant that opens with the sun and when it transforms into a wonderful round ball of seeds, it sends its wishes out into the world.

My uncle made dandelion wine. He left this world before we could verify how he made dandelion wine or ask him about the taste. What I remember is that he made dandelion wine. I've asked family members what they remember but it seems that the memories and the facts have faded with time or are unknown.

Meditation with Dandelions and Pineapples

My brother grew a pineapple, or at least the leaves of the plant. We did not have plants in the house except for this pineapple plant. One day, it was thrown out. I think our mother thought it was dead. Perhaps it was, as I did not see it grow and I did not look after it. It was just there – in a large planter's pot. My brother married and left the pineapple plant at the house. What I remember is that I did not have a relationship with it – it was just there until it wasn't. To the best of my memory, we did not talk to the plant to help it grow and produce a pineapple. I think if we did talk to the plant back in the '50s, people would have looked at us funny. Would it have ever produced a pineapple? Maybe. I understand that it takes two years or more to grow a pineapple and care is needed. They are not like dandelions, which can grow anywhere and in almost any condition.

Pineapples have a place on this planet and, given the right conditions, the plant will produce a delicious fruit with health benefits. Dandelions also have a place and they too have benefits. The floral yellow flower is one of the first signs of spring. It is the season after a cold winter and before the warmth of summer. It is a sign of new beginnings and transformations.

Everyone, everything, every memory, every truth, every word has a place in this universe. Sometimes people fall through the cracks in any family, system, or organization. We see a situation or event as broken and cannot be repaired. However, the cracks or gaps allow us to reflect upon our behaviour and reflect upon what is really happening. Meditation helps us to refocus on what is important and will help us find a way to build a bridge in our relationships and to close the gap. Meditation will help us to stay connected and form new beginnings.

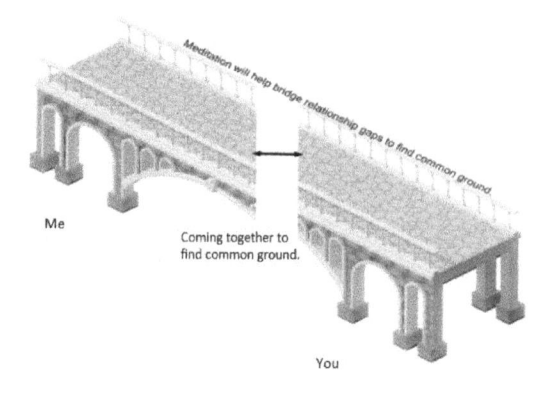

Me

Coming together to find common ground.

You

Meditation with Dandelions and Pineapples

Nature/Tea Focus
Dandelion

The dandelion is adaptable and flexible, and changes as it grows. Every part of the dandelion is important. The plant is full of vitamins and minerals. It has health benefits and may be effective in the treatment of high blood pressure. Dandelion leaves are used to add flavour to salads, sandwiches, and teas. The roots are used for drinks and the flowers can be used to make wines. Dandelion root tea can have a soothing effect on the root chakra.

The dandelion is a perennial plant that has dark green leaves, a deep taproot, and a hollow stem. They are often seen as weeds and a nuisance; however, they do have medicinal properties and are symbolically seen as hope, growth, and healing.

Dandelions burst through the ground after a long and hard winter. They are survivors. They are strong. Their yellow flowers, shaped like the sun, display a blanket of yellow on the ground. Days after they flower, dandelions burst into moon-shaped fluffy puffballs, spreading their seeds everywhere. The seeds do not discern where they will grow and plant their roots, as dandelions can be found in cracks of cement sidewalks. The life of a dandelion appears to be short, as they are seen as weeds and mowed down, but in reality they may live ten years or longer.

Pineapple

The pineapple is a fruit and resembles a pine cone. The large, oval fruit is sweet and is white or yellow in colour with a spiky outer shell and a fibrous inner core. It is neither a pine cone nor an apple. It is a group of berries that have grown together. It can take more than two years to grow one pineapple. It is known for its medicinal properties. The pineapple is used symbolically to show hospitality and a welcoming nature.

Dandelion Tea

You can make dandelion tea from the leaves, flowers, and roots of the plant. Tea made with the flowers tends to be more delicate and sweeter than tea made with the roots and leaves.

Fill a pot with 4 cups (1 L) of water and a half a quart of fresh, chopped dandelion flowers and leaves. Bring the water to a boil and let steep for about ten to twenty minutes, depending on the preferred strength. Strain and sweeten. Serve hot or cold.

Option: Put the dandelion leaves into a tea ball or infuser and let steep for about ten minutes.

Dandelion Flower Tea

Gather the yellow blossoms. Rinse well to make sure there are no residual chemicals, dirt, or insects. You will need approximately a half cup of flower buds, loosely packed, for every cup of dandelion tea. Warm the tea pot first with hot water and discard after a minute. Pour hot boiling water into the tea pot. Place the flowers into a tea strainer or use tea bags and put the flowers into the hot water. Let steep for approximately ten minutes. Sweeten, if desired.

Pineapple Tea

Pineapple tea is an anti-inflammatory drink. To make the tea, do not throw out the skin. Save all the scraps from the pineapple. Clean them in a vinegar bath for about thirty minutes, rinse, and then put all the ingredients into a pot to boil for thirty minutes. Strain and serve hot or cold. This delicious drink may be stored in the refrigerator for approximately one week.

4 cups (1 L) water
1 stick of cinnamon
1 knob of ginger (5 cm or 2 inches long)
¼ teaspoon turmeric
1-2 tablespoon (15-30 ml) maple syrup

Spill the Tea on Meditation

If it is out of your hands, it deserves freedom from your mind too.

Unknown

Journal

Meditation with Dandelions and Pineapples

Never be in a hurry; do everything calmly and quietly. Do not lose your inner peace for anything or anyone, even if your whole world seems to be in chaos.

Unknown

Journal

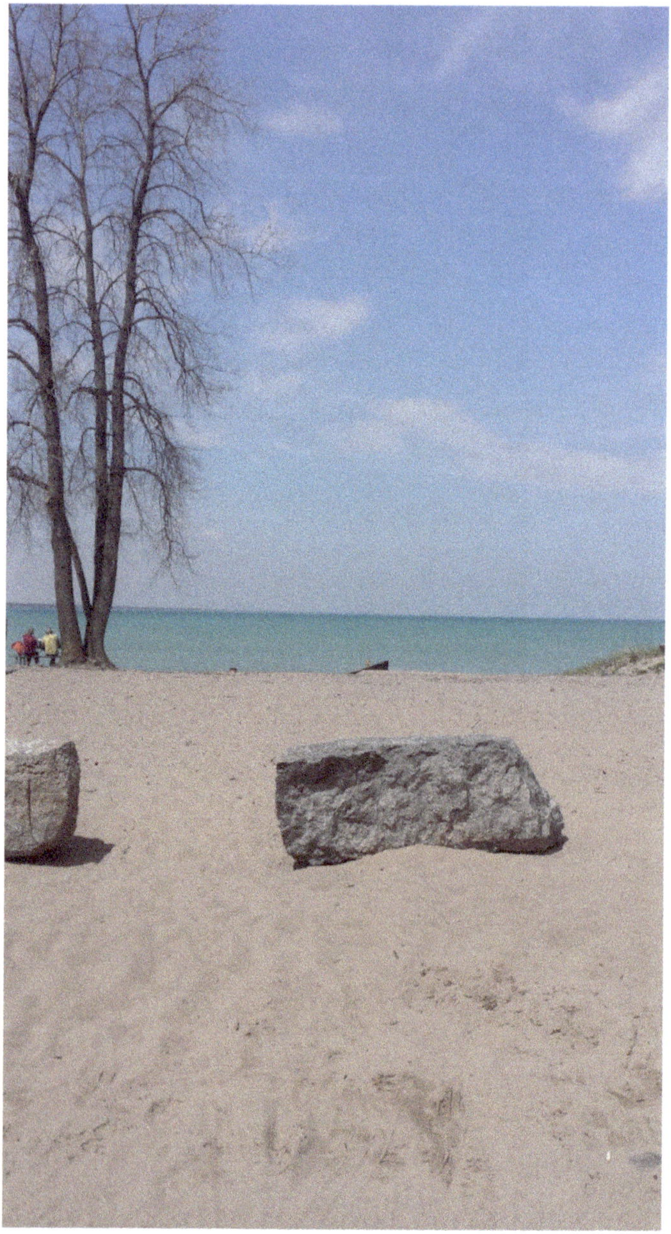

Meditation with Calendula and Mint

Journal Prompts & Self-Reflection Questions

Affirmations

Tea & Meditation

My Musings

Nature/Tea Focus—Calendula and Mint Tea

Setting your Soul Intentions

Every person, every thing is created with the same elements as the universe. To honour another is to honour the universe and its divine creator. Your soul intention comes from a deep desire to participate in and with life. *What is your deepest desire? What do you desire to do in this very moment?* Setting your intention will draw you to people, places, and opportunities that will help shape your future. You may want to focus your intentions on health, finances, or relationships. Imagine your intention as if it is already present. Visualize the people, events, feelings, and emotions that support your intention. Close your eyes and see your intention being revealed to you right now – in the present moment. As you go through your day become aware of the positives and any negatives you experience. Replace the negatives with positive thoughts, feelings, and words that support your intention. Create a touchstone at your door to help you focus on what you want to experience today. Create your story!

Butterfly

I began as starlight,
One with this planet,
A seed planted somewhere ready to begin its journey.
Learning.
Changing.
Many blessings to be discovered.
A caterpillar moving along.
Perhaps oblivious to the blessings of life.
Climbing the mountain and following others.
I learn.
I change.
So many gifts unopened.
I experience the pain of the journey.
Wanting to release the arrow that causes suffering.
Wanting to hide within my home.
My chrysalis.
It's not time.
I continue the journey.
I wait.
Still learning.
Still changing.

Maureen Lowden

Journal Prompts & Self-Reflection Questions

(Use this space to journal and self-reflect)

> ***What am I filling my life up with?*** Do you find yourself too busy? Do you find your daily schedule is too busy and you have to cancel or reschedule? Does completing a certain task make you feel important? Does a task fill you with a sense of self-worth or do you feel a sense of pride? Is what you are doing more important than your self-worth? Learning to deal with busyness and thinking there is not enough time in the day can become the norm. When you are not busy, when you think you have a moment, take some time to relax, pause, take in a deep breath, and become comfortable with the feeling. Pivot when you can from being busy to Being and enjoy your journey.

Are you reflective and able to detach from the fear of looking inwards?

_____

_____

_____

_____

_____

_____

_____

What will you see?

_____

_____

_____

_____

_____

What will you feel?

_____

_____

_____

_____

What do you think you will experience when you look inward?

_____

_____

_____

_____

_____

Affirmations

Trust the Universe

Affirmation	I am my truth.
_____	I love and trust myself.
_____	I give myself time to heal.
_____	I choose to be the light within the darkness.
_____	I am in charge of my happiness.
_____	I am joyful.
	I welcome abundance and prosperity into my life.
Visualization	I think with my heart and love with my mind.
_____	I am free to choose.
_____	I know my boundaries.
_____	I am intuitive.
_____	I am expressive.
	I am loved.
	I release control of things I
Intention / Action Plan	cannot accept. I let go of what I cannot change.
_____	I trust the Universe is working for the good of all.
_____	I trust the journey and the process.
_____	
_____	

Have enough courage to trust love one more time and always one more time.

Maya Angelou

Tea & MEditation

Find a comfortable seated position where you will not be disturbed. Take a deep breath in through your nose and exhale through your mouth. Relax your shoulders, your facial muscles, and your neck. Stay focused on your breath. You might want to close your eyes. Breathe at a pace that is relaxed for you. There is no rush. Sense within you the rise and fall of your chest. The time is now, this moment. Release any thoughts or stresses that come to you. Allow yourself to pause and breathe as you transition away from what you were doing prior to this moment. Know you are safe. Sense the natural way your breath travels throughout the body. Notice the rise of your chest with each inhale and on the exhale release any stress in your body. Scan your body where there is stress or pain and breathe into those areas. On your next breath, breathe in for a count of three and exhale for a count for three. Use a count that feels comfortable and natural for you. Breathe in and out without effort and relax into this feeling.

Ask yourself a soul searching question: *What do I want? What am I grateful for?* Relax with your question and let go of any answers that come to you. Pause for a moment and reflect on any answers. There are no right or wrong answers and if an answer is not coming or if your intuition is quiet, accept the quietness as an answer. Take in a few deep breaths to quiet your thoughts. Say the mantra, *So Hum. I am.* Repeat the mantra for a few moments.

Breathe with a pace that is comfortable and steady for you. Release the mantra *So Hum* and silently say the mantra, *Sat Chit Ananda.**

Truth-Knowingness-Bliss. Repeat the mantra a few times and then let it go. Rest in this space for a few moments remembering that our very first breath was an inhale and our last breath will be an exhale. The moment is now.

When you are ready, return to a relaxed breathing pattern. If you sense a desire to control your breath, simply acknowledge it, and return to the natural flow. Keeping your eyes closed, release any tension you feel in your body. Visualize the tension leaving your body out through your feet and grounding you to the earth.

As you open your eyes, give thanks and send love and healing out to the world. Stay with this feeling for as long as possible. Hydrate. Pour yourself a cup of tea and enjoy. Namaste.

*Sat Chit Ananda - Discovering or acknowledging the inner nature of your soul.

Meditation with Calendula and Mint

Mere colour can speak to the soul in a thousand different ways.

Oscar Wilde

Tea & MEditation

Find a place that is comfortable where you can relax. You may want to lie down or have a chair that supports your head. Be ready to close your eyes. Your mind is open and free. Take a deep breath in to the count of four and breathe out to a count of four. Feel your body getting lighter. Breathe in to a count of four and breathe out to a count of four. Return to your normal breathing.

Sense you are safe and supported in your journey. Focus on your breathing if your thoughts become distracting. Again, breathe in to a count of four and breathe out to a count of four. Clear the area of any negative energy. Imagine there is a golden sheet on the ground and you are gradually lifting it up, bringing any negative energy up with it and leaving a rainbow of colours below. You feel peaceful and calm. As you gradually lift the sheet over your head, send it off to the sun. Feel the sun's warmth on your skin. Sense the sun's light through your closed eyes.

You are safe and supported. Ground yourself to the earth. The energy flowing from your feet is connecting deep into the planet. Rest here for a moment. Visualize a golden inner light in your heart centre. Allow this golden light to shower the colours of pink and green over you as it flows from your heart centre to your upper chest, to the back and front of your neck, to the base of your skull, up to your crown chakra, and out. Release your jaw and relax your eyes. Rest here with the calming colours for as long as you wish.

As you breathe, allow the colours to surround your physical body and your heart centre. You are safe. You are loved. When you are ready, move your toes and fingers. Gradually awaken your body and allow your positive thoughts of self-love to be present. Send love out to the world, to friends, family, to everyone on the planet. Hydrate.

Pour yourself a cup of tea and enjoy your day.

Namaste.

Meditation with Calendula and Mint

There is always light. If only we are brave enough to see it. If only we are brave enough to be it.

Amanda Gorman

My Musings

I came across the calendula flower while I was taking an essential oil course. I collect dried herbs, fruits, and flowers to make a pot of tea and a friend gave me some dried calendula from her garden. Calendula in some cultures is a symbol of endurance. Its story also extends to joy, remembrance, prosperity, and protection.

Drinking a warm cup of tea helps me to slow down, relax, and connect with the vibrational energy level of my situation. I keep clear quartz crystals near my tea leaves to help clear any negative energy. Slowing down, taking time to reflect, focusing on my breath, enjoying a cup of tea, and meditating helps me to remember that love is real. Genuine love transforms your behaviour to one that is caring and wanting the best for another – for them to be well and happy. Meditation helps to transform and heal. We may not perceive any changes in our energy flow but change occurs. Meditation will change the flow of energy we bring to a situation. It might simply be a change in our breathing pattern, or our thoughts quietening, or our heart rate slowing down. We can feel the change within when we focus on our breathing and allow the energy level to be transformed. We can change hate to love, sadness to joy, impatience to patience, scared to confident, embarrassed to acceptance, attachment to detachment and letting go to allow change to occur.

Small children usually ask lots of questions and sometimes adults, parents, and caregivers do not have the answers. "Why is the sky blue?" Why do the leaves turn beautiful colours in autumn? Why do I see clouds? Why is the water cold? As an adult, my questions grew deeper. What is life about on this planet? What do I fear? What are my gifts? Why did this happen to me? Why is there a dual nature? What is the lesson I am supposed to learn? Questions are useful as they open communication between people. Questions help us to understand our own beliefs and ideas as well as the priorities and beliefs of others, and questions can help motivate us to explore our creativity.

I remember a peaceful time when the family would stroll along the street or in the park and our 3-year old daughter would ask questions. Her questions always started with "Why?" I remember the answer we finally gave her, "Because the sun rises in the East and sets in the West." We knew it was not the best answer as she continued to ask, "Why?" but some answers would be quite complicated. Perhaps our response would eventually allow her to explore and discover the science behind the questions. When you're tired though sometimes the response is given without thinking and the fact that it just is, is the easiest response. I often ask questions in prayer or when I am self-reflective. Maybe our answer to our daughter's questions was not too far off the mark. I think the best answer to all my questions about life is witnessing life being born, watching the miracle of the sunrise and the sunset, and realizing my day begins and ends with the beauty of nature. What a lovely way to start and end your day.

Nature/Tea Focus

Calendula

Calendula is also known as the *pot marigold;* however, the plant is not related to regular garden marigolds. It has been around for thousands of years. Calendula is a wonderful garden plant. Bees and native pollinators are drawn to these bright beautiful flowers. It is thought that calendula repels many pests which is a bonus for gardeners.

Calendula and Peppermint Teas

Calendula Tea

Calendula is a beneficial and versatile herb that is perfect for tea. Calendula has a sweet fragrance but a slightly bitter taste. If you want a sweeter tea, add a bit of honey.

You can use fresh calendula blossoms (about four flowers per person) in a teapot. Pour boiling water into a teapot, add the fresh blossoms, and steep for three to four minutes. Strain, add honey if desired.

If you use dried calendula petals, add one to two tablespoons (15 to 30 ml) into a teabag or infuser and place the petals into a teapot or a cup of boiling water. Allow to steep for three to four minutes. Add honey if desired.

Note: You can add other flavours and herbs to your calendula tea. I like adding fresh ginger and lemon. Create your own blend of tea as calendula will add flavour. I enjoy Earl Grey tea with calendula. Chamomile and peppermint are also delicious with calendula.

Peppermint Tea

The mint plants are perennial plants and very hardy. Mint tea is usually made from peppermint leaves but you can add spearmint leaves for a refreshing taste.

Peppermint tea is free of calories and caffeine. You can use fresh or dried leaves. To make peppermint tea, boil two cups of water and then turn off the heat. Add the peppermint leaves or any mint leaves to the water and steep for approximately four to five minutes. If desired, add a slice of ginger. Strain the tea into your favourite cup and enjoy.

By itself, peppermint tea is delicious and cooling. If you enjoy a sweeter tea, add a little honey. You can enjoy mint tea all day, every day, but you might want to set a limit of two to three cups daily.

Calendula-Infused Oil

Ingredients:
Organic calendula flowers
Olive oil or an oil of your choice

Directions:
Fill a glass jar two thirds (2/3) of the way full with dried calendula flowers.
Pour oil into the jar, making sure to cover the flowers so they will have space to expand.
Stir well and cap the jar tightly.
Place the jar somewhere warm and shake once a day.
After one or two weeks, strain the herbs out using cheesecloth.
Pour the infused oil into a glass bottle and store in a cool, dark place.

Calendula oil can be worked into the scalp and helps with dry skin.

Peppermint

Peppermint is a natural mint herbal plant that grows wild. You might even have some in the garden or as a house plant. It is a healthy and sturdy plant. The herb has been used for hundreds of years for flavouring and for its possible medicinal properties to help with digestion, sleep, and fresher breath.

Meditation with Calendula and Mint

We don't create abundance. Abundance is always present. We create limitations. Remove those and you'll attract all that you desire.

Arnold M. Patent

Journal

It is during our darkest moments that we must focus to see the light.

Aristotle

Journal

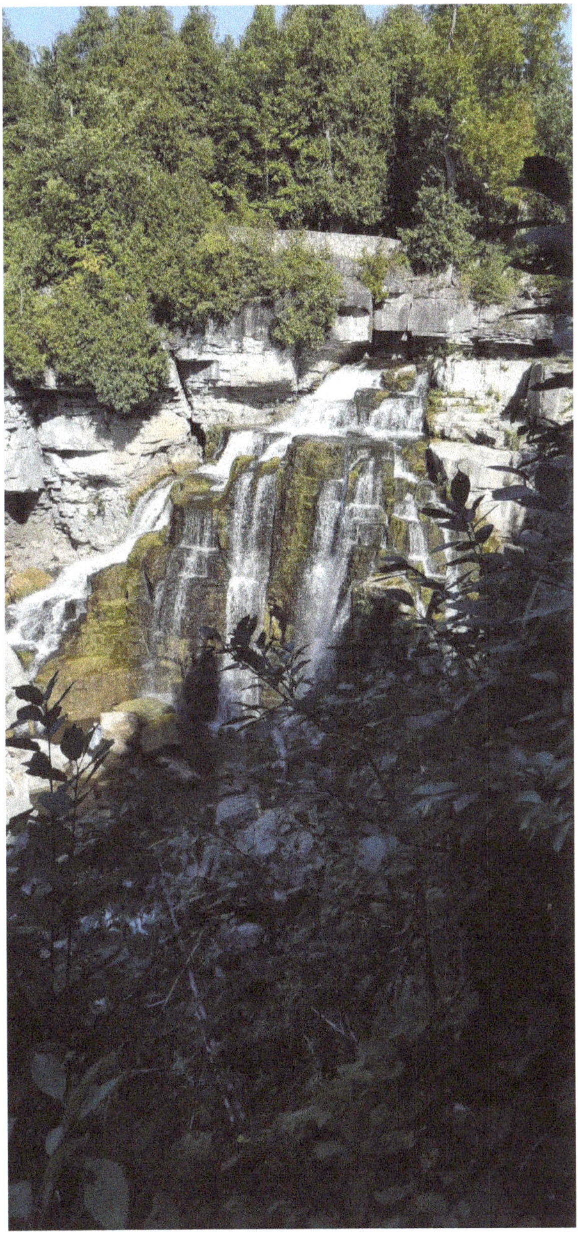

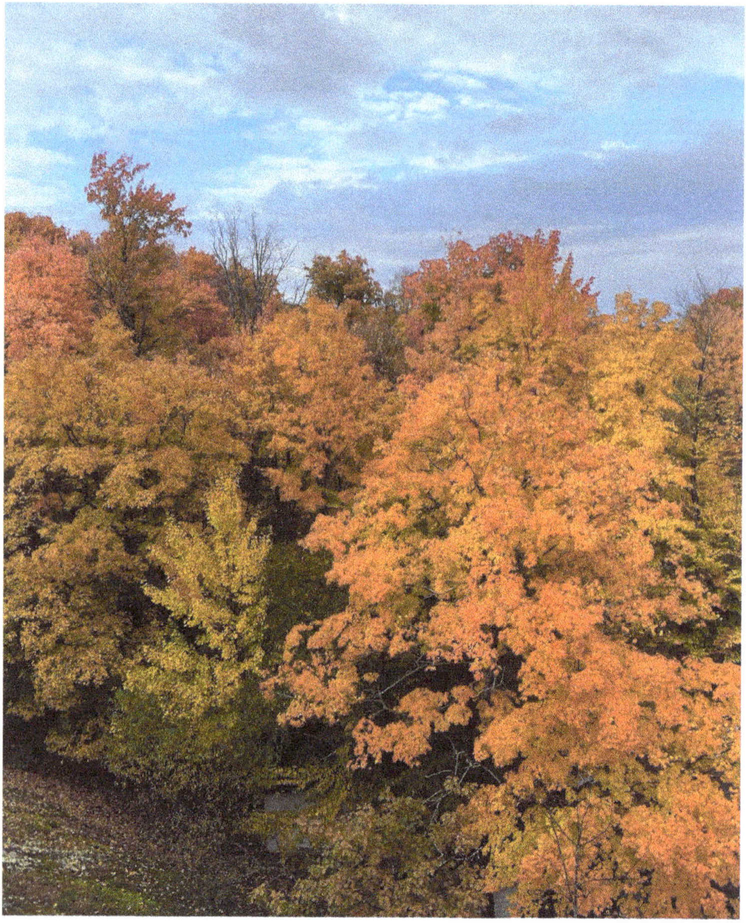

Meditation with Maple

Journal Prompts & Self-Reflection Questions

Affirmations

Tea & MEditation

My Musings

Nature/Tea Focus—Maple

Chanting: A chant is a repeated rhythmic phrase that is sung in a repetitive tone. It is an ancient practice and helps to raise our physiology and vibration level. According to Albert Einstein, *everything in life is vibration.* The love frequency of 528Hz is thought to connect everything – our heart, our spiritual nature, and the Divine. Chanting can decrease stress, anxiety, and depression symptoms. It can increase a feeling of relaxation and bring about a positive mood change. Chants, mantras, and tones are ways to focus our attention and help to increase our awareness. The Gregorian chants are beautiful chants and are capable of healing hearts and bringing happiness to those who listen.

I want to sing like the birds,
not caring who listens or what they think.

Rumi

Spill the Tea on Meditation

Circle of Life

Trees
Life
showing its beauty
roots grounding deep
into the earth
covering above as below
the sun shining its glory
the wind shifting its warmth
the emeralds are changing
shimmering of diamonds, rubies, topaz
fairies sitting upon each leaf
glistening in the sun's rays
listening to the rustling leaves
floating
falling on the ground
a coat of many colours
striped of its bloom
the tree shows life and strength
ready for new growth
another circle of life.

Maureen Lowden

Journal Prompts & Self-Reflection Questions

(Use this space to journal and self-reflect)

> What goodness/joy do I want more of in my life? Life loves us all. Staying centred is sometimes difficult. Staying happy and joyful is sometimes even more difficult. Whenever I experience emotions and feelings that do not bring joy, I realize these feelings and emotions are temporary and part of this world I live in. It seems to be the duality of nature—being in the world and Being of the world. You have all the time in the world to create the life you desire, so let go of your need to control.
>
> *The unstoppable spirit of renewal is in you. Trust it.*
> *Learn that it flows through you and all of life.*
>
> *Jack Kornfield*

Past experiences keep presenting themselves in the present moment. Is the present moment filled with unconditional love for yourself?

_____

_____

_____

_____

_____

_____

_____

There are no wrong choices, just choices. I will not let my choices be controlled by others or control my life and my joy. Does this statement speak to you?

Affirmations

Courage and Bravery

Affirmation	I have everything I need to be successful.
	I am assertive.
	Goodness flows to me and through me.
	Love is my power.
	I am open and willing to live my life in new ways.
Visualization	I am a vibrant and energetic being.
	I am brilliant.
	I am creative.
	I am inspired.
	I am brave.
	I am divinely led through difficult situations.
	I surrender all expectations.
Intention / Action Plan	I am open to receive.
	I hand over my concerns to the universe.

Kindness in words creates confidence. Kindness in thinking creates profoundness. Kindness in giving creates love.

Lao Tzu

Tea & MEditation

Affirmation: Love holds space for all experiences.

Consciously connect to your breath. Take a moment to connect and feel your breath flowing in and throughout your body. Visualize your breath flowing to your feet and to the top of your head. It feels good to relax and allow your breath to flow in and out. Place your hand over your heart centre and rest. If you feel any pain from this life or past lives, witness the pain with compassion and love and let it flow out with your breath.

Visualize light at your heart centre and let it encompass and flow within your whole body. Allow your love for yourself to become strong and nourishing.

Repeat the affirmation: Love holds space for all experiences.

Rest in this loving visualization you have created for as long as you wish. You are safe. You are loved.

When you are ready move your toes and fingers. Gradually awaken your body and allow your positive thoughts of self-love to be present. Send love out to the world and hold your family, friends, and community in loving thoughts. Hydrate.

Pour yourself a cup of tea and enjoy your day. Namaste.

Spill the Tea on Meditation

You just love until you and the beloved become one.

Ram Dass

Tea & MEditation

Find a quiet place where you will not be interrupted. Place your hands in your lap with palms facing up. Focus on your breathing. Breathe in through your nose and out through your mouth. When you exhale, send out any negative energy. Scan your body and, where you feel stress, release it. Focus on the area where you feel discomfort and let it go. Continue to breathe normally.

When you are ready, breathe in and when you are breathing out, slowly move your head and neck to your right shoulder, raising your shoulder to meet your head. Rest for a moment and breathe.

On the inhale, slowly return your head to centre. On the exhale, slowly move your head to your left shoulder, raising your shoulder to meet your head. Rest here for a moment.

On the inhale, slowly return your head to centre. On the exhale, slowly lower your head to your chest. Rest here for a moment.

On the inhale, slowly raise your head. On the exhale, slowly tilt your head slightly back and then on the inhale, slowly raise your head back to centre. Rest here for a moment.

On the inhale, slowly raise both shoulders to your ears and then on the exhale lower your shoulders. Do this two more times.

On the inhale, slowly round up and pull your shoulders back and on the exhale, return your shoulders to a normal position. Do this two more times.

On the inhale, slowly round up and roll your shoulders forward and on the exhale, return your shoulders to a normal position. Do this two more times.

Focus on breathing deeply.

Silently focus on the soul intentions. I have a calm and understanding nature. My body is healthy and strong. My mind is open and reflective. I am love.

Visualize a pond and as you come closer you throw a pebble into the water. You watch the pebble enter the water and see the ripple effect flow outward. The pebble is your intention and you are watching the flow of energy move outwards.

I have a calm and understanding nature. My body is healthy and strong. My mind is open and reflective. I am love.

When you are ready, slowly open your eyes. Send love and forgiveness out to the whole world.

Hydrate. Pour yourself a cup of tea. Namaste.

Don't be ashamed to weep; 'tis right to grieve. Tears are only water, and flowers, trees, and fruit cannot grow without water. But there must be sunlight also. A wounded heart will heal in time, and, when it does, the memory and love of our lost ones is sealed inside to comfort us.

Brian Jacques, Taggerung

My Musings

We receive signs every day that may help guide us in our daily activities. We need to trust our senses and have faith that we are being guided on the right path. I love the maple tree. I see signs of it everywhere whether it is a branch fallen to the ground near me, the maple keys twirling in the air, or a leaf that has drifted toward me. One day I was sitting in the park and a small green maple leaf floated down from the tree and landed in front of me. Another day, a maple leaf landed right on my car window.

The maple tree is a symbol of strength and protection. In some countries it is an ancient symbol of love and longevity. It is a tree that keeps on giving and has been doing so for millions of years. The sap represents the sweetness and wonder of love in daily life. The sap is the life blood of the tree and from the sap, maple syrup is produced.

Chlorophyll saturates the leaves making them appear green. The green we see is the result of photosynthesis in plants and trees. It is the process to transform sunlight, water, and carbon dioxide to create oxygen and energy in the form of sugar molecules. When the days become shorter, the process of photosynthesis slows down with the effect that the green leaves transform into the brilliant colours of orange, yellow, and red. The beta carotene (orange), anthocyanin (red) and flavonol (yellow) which were masked by the chlorophyll are now seen. Transformation

– a dramatic change from green to vibrant colours. That which was hidden is now seen.

The maple tree has provided many gifts - shade, coolness, colour, fallen leaves, maple syrup, and maple flavoured food and water. I have tried other tree syrups like birch, beech, and others but, to me, none seem to have the sweetness and goodness of the maple tree sap.

The maple leaf is Canada's symbol on the national flag. I actually did not think it was a good idea back in the 'sixties' to change the Canadian flag but now I see the wisdom of having a flag that represents Canada's long history with the maple leaf.

When the design of Canada's flag was presented to Canadians I was not aware of the historical significance of the symbol. I am a daughter of two WWII veterans who fought under Canada's Red Ensign. To WWI veterans and military personal, the maple leaf was already a symbol of Canada. It was worn as a cap badge by service men and women and displayed on equipment. Canadian Olympic and hockey uniforms featured a maple leaf design. It was carved upon many headstones of Canadian service men and women. The maple leaf is a symbol on coins and shared in books, songs, and many other items. It also represents Canada's vast natural resources.

When the Red Ensign was lowered at noon on February 15, 1965, and the new National Flag of Canada was hoisted, Canada's Prime Minister Pearson spoke the words, *May the land over which this new flag flies remain united in freedom and justice ... sensitive, tolerant and compassionate toward all.*

Nature/Tea Focus
Maple Tree

There are over one hundred species of the maple tree and the tree has been on this planet for over 100 million years. The sap of any tree is its life line. The sap of the maple tree has a higher sugar content than other trees and it is what gives the syrup, candies, cookies, and other types of food its distinctive taste. A maple tree symbolizes a promise of balance, love, longevity, protection, and abundance.

Maple Iced Green Tea

Ingredients
1 cup (250 ml) boiling water
4 green* tea bags or 4 teaspoons (20 ml)
½ cup (125 ml) pure maple syrup
6 cups (1½ L) water
1 lemon

Directions:
Boil 1 cup (250 ml) of water and add 4 green tea bags. Add ½ cup (125 ml) pure maple syrup and let the mixture steep for five minutes. Remove the tea bags and allow the tea to cool. In a pitcher, combine 6 cups (1 ½ L) of water, maple green tea, and the juice of one lemon. Mix well and refrigerate.

*Note: If you prefer to use a black tea, the drink will be just as delicious. Use a good quality loose leaf black tea.

Maple Water

I recently discovered maple water. It is thirst quenching and delicious. Add one teaspoon (5 ml) of maple syrup to a glass of cold or hot water and stir. If you desire a stronger and sweeter maple flavour, add more maple syrup.

Meditation with Maple

Life has a way of presenting you with the perfect people to align with who can give you a leg up during your next phase of your journey. Help comes to you in all areas of your life where you need a boost.

Colette Baron-Reid

Journal

_____

_____

_____

_____

_____

_____

_____

_____

_____

_____

_____

_____

_____

_____

_____

Spill the Tea on Meditation

You may not consider yourself a creative person, but in fact you are creating your reality every moment of every day via your thoughts, feelings, beliefs, intentions, and actions. You must consider that you do so in partnership with Spirit, Consciousness, God, or whatever name you call your Higher Power.

Colette Baron-Reid

Journal

Major Chakra Centres

Crown Chakra,
Spirituality

Third Eye Chakra
Awareness

Throat Chakra,
Communication

Heart Chakra,
Love, Healing

Solar Plexus
Chakra,
Wisdom, Power

Sacral Chakra
Sexuality, Creativity

Root Chakra
Basic Trust

Major Chakra Centres and Spiritual Modalities

The word chakra refers to various energy centres, circles, or energy wheels in your body that correspond to specific nerve bundles and internal organs. They are akin to acupuncture points in your body. The seven main chakras move up your spinal cord beginning with the first chakra located at the base of the spine to the seventh chakra located at the top of the head. There are over a hundred chakra centres in the human body that are divided into minor and micro chakras that are just as important, however, they are not as well known.

Chakra centres hold bundles of nerves and organs as well as psychological, emotional, and spiritual states of being. The chakras are essential for connecting you to the vastness of the universe and to your authentic self. Each chakra centre governs different aspects of your life. The seven main chakras are the Root or Base Chakra (relating to security and basic survival needs), Sacral and Solar Plexus Chakras (relating to matters such as emotions, feelings, sexuality, and power), Throat Chakra (speaking your truth), Third Eye, Crown and

> **Seven Main Chakras**
>
> **Root Chakra** - located at the base of the spine
>
> **Sacral Chakra** - located at the root of the sexual organs approximately three fingers below the navel
>
> **Solar Plexus Chakra** - located at the navel
>
> **Heart Chakra** - located within the centre of the chest
>
> **Throat Chakra** - located at the throat
>
> **Third Eye Chakra** - located at the forehead, between the eyebrows
>
> **Crown Chakra** - located at the top of the head

Heart Chakras (bridging the two worlds -physical and spiritual- with love and compassion).

The Alta Major Chakra is a chakra (relating to higher consciousness, truth, intuition, and purpose) and is located at the base of the skull. Its energy flows throughout the body bridging the mind, body, and heart. It may be considered the eighth chakra.

The body and mind are complex systems processing every thought, memory, touch, sight, smell, emotion, feeling, and experience. It is important that the energy centres be aligned and fluid. The intention is to clear the chakra centres in the body to help energy flow allowing the body, mind, and spirit to become balanced.

Chakra healing is the intentional practice to connect with our inner reality to heal and to help us better understand our past, present actions, and reactions. When the chakras are open, energy flows freely through the physical body and mind. Each chakra is connected with the physical body, as well as with our emotions and feelings. There is a wide range of ways to unblock, clear, align, and open the chakras. One way to open and balance the body's energy centres is through a healthy diet as well as meditation, crystals, and sound.

The chakras are associated with a colour, a stone or gem, an element, a symbol, essential oils and a bija or sound. A bija is a one-syllable sound that, when chanted, activates the energy of the chakra in order to purify and balance the mind and body. Each chakra has its own frequency or vibration that resonates as its life force.

When a chakra is blocked, the physical body and mind are not aligned and operating at full potential. To clear a chakra centre begin the mantra with the bija or seed sound and chant the sounds related to the blocked chakra - *LAM* (root), *VAM* (sacral), *RAM* (solar plexus), *YAM* (heart), *HAM* (throat), *OM* (third eye and crown).

Solfeggio frequencies are an ancient scale of healing tones that relate to healing. The tones are said to have been created by a Benedictine monk and are used in chants by Gregorian monks. Listening to music created in one of the frequencies on this scale will evoke healing. The main solfeggio frequencies are – 396 Hz for healing from fear and guilt, 417 Hz for facilitating change and healing trauma, 528 Hz for clarity, peace, and repair of cells and tissues, 639 Hz to heal relationships and restore balance, 741 Hz finding solutions, heal communication, and eliminate negativity, 852 Hz to awaken intuition and restore to balance the mind, body, soul, and spirit, and 963 Hz to help raise energy and to manifest positive situations and outcomes. Newer frequencies have been added to the scale - 174 Hz (healing the physical body), 285 Hz (heals and restores tissues and is associated with the root chakra), 396 Hz (heals and transforms feelings of grief, guilt and doubt to a state of positivity).

The Universe and everything on the planet is vibrating, oscillating, and resonating at different frequencies. Sound waves were heard by the Planck space telescope as a constant humming. This humming has been translated into frequencies we can hear. The sound frequencies can be used in meditation to bring peace, healing, and calmness. The mantra *Om* is the first primordial sound and is used to bring stillness and silence.

Spiritual modalities such as prayer, meditation, chakras, music, mantras, and chants help a person achieve a higher level of awareness. Enjoying a cup of tea can also be a pathway to a higher level of awareness as the ritual allows you to step away from the hustle and bustle of life and enter stillness, self-awareness, and self-reflection.

Major Chakra Centres, Associated Properties, and Frequencies

Root Chakra Muladhara "The root of all things" base of spine, at the tailbone	Bija/Seed mantra: LAM Intent: I Am – strong, at peace feeling of safety and security, liberate fear, guilt, trauma Sense: Smell	Energy: survival, belonging, security Element: Earth Frequency: 432Hz, solfeggio 396Hz Colour: Red
Sacral Chakra Swadhisthana "The creation/ social chakra" centre of lower belly	Bija/Seed mantra: VAM Intent: I Feel - creativity flowing, help with creative visualization, opens the mind to accept change Sense: Taste	Energy: creativity, sexuality, pleasure Element: Water Frequency: 480Hz, solfeggio 417Hz Colour: Orange
Solar Plexus Chakra Manipura "City of Jewels" upper belly at the diaphragm	Bija/Seed mantra: RAM Intent: I Do - let go of control, let go of the past, help with personal power and confidence, transformation Sense: Sight	Energy: willpower, motivation, self-esteem Element: Fire Frequency: 528Hz, solfeggio 528Hz Colour: Yellow
Heart Chakra Anahata "Unhurt" centre of the spine, heart	Bija/Seed mantra: YAM Intent: I Love – with compassion and understanding, healing relationships, interpersonal connections Sense: Touch	Energy: love, compassion Element: Air Frequency: 594Hz, solfeggio 639Hz Colour: Green and Pink

Major Chakra Centres

Throat Chakra Vishuddha "Individual Truth" centre of neck	Bija/Seed mantra: HAM Intent: I Speak - my words with truth, my words are like seeds, associated with communication and empathy, finding solutions Sense: Hearing	Energy: expression, physical-spiritual voice Element: Ether Frequency: 672Hz, solfeggio 741Hz Colour: Light Blue
Third Eye Chakra Ajna "The seat of intuition" centre of forehead, brow	Bija/Seed mantra: OM Intent: I See - I am open to new ideas, restoring connections, bringing spiritual order Sense: Intuition	Energy: wisdom, guidance Element: Light Frequency: 720Hz, solfeggio 852Hz Colour: Indigo, Dark Blue
Crown Chakra Sahasrara "The bridge to the cosmos" top of skull	Bija/Seed mantra: AUM or listening Intent: I understand - surrender to the highest power, connection with higher consciousness Sense: Beyond the senses	Energy: spirituality, knowledge, fulfillment Element: Thought/Space Frequency: 768 Hz, solfeggio 963Hz Colour: Violet, Purple, White
Alta Major Chakra "Mouth of God/Goddess" base of the skull	Bija/Seed mantra: OM or listening Intent: Divine inspiration and intuition	Energy: balancing the mind, body, heart Element: Union Frequency: 768Hz Colour: Teal, Blue/Green

*Solfeggio Frequencies promote healing

If you believe the phrase you are what you think, then life truly stems from your thoughts. But we cannot rely purely on thoughts; we must translate thoughts into words and eventually into actions in order to manifest our intentions. This means we have to be very careful with our words, choosing to speak only those which work toward our benefit and cultivate our highest good.

Dr. Carmen Harra

Alta Major Chakra

located at the base of the skull
at the back of the neck by the brain stem and branches out into the brain
The mantra for the Alta Major chakra is OM.
Element: Connecting to peace, protection, strength
Colours: magenta, teal (blue for expansion and growth, green for healing)

The alta major chakra was known by ancient cultures as the *Mouth of God/Goddess* - the path to ascension - the seat of consciousness.

This chakra connects the pineal and pituitary glands, thymus, crown, and heart chakra. Its energy reaches down through the spine, disperses throughout the body and branches up to the crown chakra. When the alta major chakra is balanced and open, you feel energized, creative, and connect with spiritual abundance and healing abilities. The colour teal is a bridge between blue and green.

MEditation

Visualize a blue, green, or teal candle glowing or visualize flowers in a field. Remember you are safe and protected and when other thoughts come, let them go and refocus on your breath.

Begin by focusing on your breath. Breathe in for a count of four, hold for a count of four, breathe out for a count of four, pause for a count of four. Repeat the breathing exercise a few times. As you continue, you may wish to extend the exhale to six and pause for six. You will begin to relax as you focus on your breath. Gently close your eyes. Visualize the colour of teal and surround yourself with the colour. Scan your body starting at the crown. If you feel any area of discomfort, gently tap the area to release any pressure. Continue scanning through your body—your eyes, jaw, ears, throat, chest, heart, arms, fingers, legs—and release any areas of discomfort. When you are ready, release the colour. Take a deep breath and relax. Chanting a mantra will help to increase your positive energy level and self-confidence and dispel negative thoughts.

Crown Chakra (Sahasrara)

located at the highest point of the body on the top of the skull
The mantra for the Crown chakra is AUM or OM or silence.
Element: thought//beyond
Energy: Spiritual and Divine connection
Connecting to higher self and the Divine
Solfeggio Sound Frequency 963Hz
Connect with the colours violet and white

The crown chakra is associated with enlightenment and wisdom. When this energy centre is open, it allows us to transcend our dual nature and become aware of our unique purpose. We may experience divine union and cosmic love. Lavender and the lotus flower assist in opening the seventh chakra. Clear quartz helps to balance and energize the chakra centres as well as to amplify other crystals. Crystals to help with balance, flow, and general connectedness are amethyst, selenite, howlite, labradorite, moonstone, and white topaz.

MEditation

Visualize a white candle glowing or violet flowers in a field. Remember, you are safe and protected and, when other thoughts come, let them go and focus on your breath.

Begin by focusing on your breath. Breathe in for a count of four, hold for a count of four, breathe out for a count of four, pause for a count of four. Repeat the breathing exercise a few times. As you continue, you may wish to extend the exhale to six and pause for six. You will begin to relax as you focus on your breath.

Quietly recite or chant the mantra *AUM*. You may wish to hold the mantra and repeat several times. Do what feels comfortable.

Chanting the mantra will help to increase your positive energy level and self-confidence and dispel negative thoughts.

Third Eye Chakra (Ajna)

located in the centre of your head, parallel to the middle of your eyebrows.
The mantra for the Third Eye chakra is OM or AUM.
Element: Light
Energy: awareness, guidance, inner vision, clear thought
Solfeggio Sound Frequency 852Hz
Connect with the colours indigo or dark blue and purple

The third eye chakra is associated with your intuition and your inner vision. It is linked to perception, awareness, and spiritual communication. Mint and jasmine are herbs used to open this chakra. Mint has been found to help with depression, migraines, and digestion, as well as energizing the third eye chakra. Crystals and gemstones that may help with our ability to see the big picture and access intuition are amethyst, labradorite, lapis lazuli, moonstone, and black tourmaline.

MEditation

You may wish to connect with the colours indigo or dark blue. Visualize a dark blue-coloured candle glowing or blue flowers in a field. Remember, you are safe and protected and, when other thoughts come, let them go and focus on your breath.

Begin by focusing on your breath. Breathe in for a count of four, hold for a count of four, breathe out for a count of four, and pause for a count of four. Repeat the breathing exercise a few times. As you continue, you may wish to extend the exhale to six and pause for six. You will begin to relax as you focus on your breath.

Quietly recite or chant the mantra *OM*. You may wish to hold the mantra and repeat several times. Do what feels comfortable.

Chanting the mantra will help to increase your positive energy level and self-confidence, bring clarity of thought, and dispel negative thoughts.

Throat Chakra (Vishuddha)

is associated with the throat region near the spine and encompasses the tongue, cheeks, jaw, and ears.
The mantra for the Throat chakra is HAM.
Element: space, ether
Energy: physical and spiritual voice, communication, self-expression, expressing your truth
Solfeggio Sound Frequency 741Hz
Connect with the colours light blue and turquoise

The throat chakra is associated with pure or purification. It is responsible for self-expression and communication. Opening the throat chakra helps our words to become uplifting allowing us to communicate our intent clearly. A red clover blossom assists with helping us to express ourselves in an authentic way without fear or anxiety. Lemon balm helps with healing the thyroid. Eucalyptus helps with decongestion. Other herbs that may help with healing are peppermint, sage, salt, and lemon grass. Sodalite, aquamarine, turquoise, and celestite crystals may help with speaking your words with truth, confidence, and love.

MEditation

You may wish to connect with the colour blue. Visualize a light blue candle glowing or light blue flowers in a field. Remember, you are safe and protected and, when other thoughts come, let them go and refocus on your breath.

Begin by focusing on your breath. Breathe in for a count of four, hold for a count of four, breathe out for a count of four, pause for a count of four. Repeat the breathing exercise a few times. As you continue, you may wish to extend the exhale to six and pause for six. You will begin to relax as you focus on your breath.

Quietly recite or chant the mantra *HAM*. You may wish to hold the mantra and repeat several times. Do what feels comfortable.

Chanting the mantra will help to increase your positive energy level and self-confidence, help with expressing your truth, and dispel negative thoughts.

Heart Chakra (Anahata)

located near your physical heart in the centre of your chest
The mantra for the Heart chakra is YAM.
Element: air or wind
Energy: compassion, affection, love
Solfeggio Sound Frequency 639Hz
Connect with the colours green and pink

The heart chakra is associated with vulnerability and intimacy. It creates the foundation for interpersonal and healthy relationships. The heart chakra is at the centre of expressing love, compassion, and forgiveness. Hawthorne berries may help to strengthen trust and the ability to love and heal ourselves. Other spices and herbs that may open the heart chakra include cayenne, jasmine, lavender, marjoram, rose, basil, sage, thyme, cilantro, and parsley. Gemstones and crystals associated with the heart chakra are emerald, malachite, jade, green aventurine, and rose quartz.

MEditation

You may wish to connect with the colour green. Visualize a green candle glowing or a field of green leaves blowing in the wind. Remember, you are safe and protected and, when other thoughts come, let them go and refocus on your breath.

Begin by focusing on your breath. Breathe in for a count of four, hold for a count of four, breathe out for a count of four, pause for a count of four. Repeat the breathing exercise a few times. As you continue, you may wish to extend the inhale and exhale to a count of six and pause for six. You will begin to relax as you focus on your breath.

Quietly recite or chant the mantra *YAM*. You may wish to hold the mantra and repeat several times. Do what feels comfortable.

Chanting the mantra may help with forgiveness, the willingness to forgive, compassion, and dispel any negative thoughts.

Solar Plexus Chakra (Manipura)

Located in the upper abdomen, at the naval
The mantra for the Solar Plexus chakra is RAM.
Element: fire
Energy: self-confidence, self-esteem, power of transformation, feeling powerful
Solfeggio Sound Frequency 528Hz
Connect with the colours yellow or gold

The solar plexus chakra is attributed to transformation, ancestral and present healing. It is the third chakra of the seven main chakras and the centre of personal strength and comprehension. When open, the flowing energy guides you through life by creating a strong sense of self. It is the power centre for our emotions and self-confidence. Lavender, bergamot, and rosemary may help to open the solar plexus chakra. Bergamot helps with the process of digestion. Earl Grey tea is infused with bergamot. Rosemary is an herb known to help with digestion. Marshmallow may help to relax the diaphragm and help with breathing. Other herbs and spices are anise, celery, cinnamon, mint, ginger, turmeric, cumin, and fennel. Crystals for the solar plexus chakra may include citrine, amber, yellow quartz, and tiger's eye and may help to manifest prosperity and positivity.

MEditation

You may wish to connect with the colour yellow. Visualize a yellow candle glowing or yellow flowers in a field. Remember, you are safe and protected and, when other thoughts come, let them go and refocus on your breath.

Begin by focusing on your breath. Breathe in for a count of four, hold for a count of four, breathe out for a count of four, pause for a count of four. Repeat the breathing exercise a few times. As you continue, you may wish to extend the exhale to six and pause for six. You will begin to relax as you focus on your breath.

Quietly recite or chant the mantra *RAM*. You may wish to hold the mantra and repeat several times. Do what feels comfortable.

Chanting the mantra may help to increase your self-confidence, strength, positive energy level, and dispel negative thoughts.

Sacral Chakra (Svadiṣṭhana)

located just below the naval (reproductive organs)
The mantra for the Sacral chakra is VAM.
Element: water
Energy: well being, creative expression,
desire for pleasure, sensuality
Solfeggio Sound Frequency 417Hz
Connect with the colour orange

The sacral chakra is associated with creativity and sensual expression. It represents vital life force, reproduction, and sexuality. It is the second of the seven main chakras and when open, has the potential to enhance relationships. Calendula enhances creativity. Gardenia is beneficial and soothing for the senses. Sandalwood may help with infection. Other herbs and spices that are beneficial for the sacral chakra include coriander, fennel, licorice, cinnamon, vanilla, carob, sweet paprika, sesame seeds, and caraway seeds. Carnelian, tiger's eye, orange calcite, sunstone and moonstone are crystals that may help with physical strength and stamina, heal emotions, and increase intuition.

Major Chakra Centres

MEditation

You may wish to connect with the colour orange. Visualize an orange candle glowing or orange flowers in a field. Remember, you are safe and protected and, when other thoughts come, let them go and refocus on your breath.

Begin by focusing on your breath. Breathe in for a count of four, hold for a count of four, breathe out for a count of four, pause for a count of four. Repeat the breathing exercise a few times. As you continue, you may wish to extend the exhale to six and pause for six. You will begin to relax as you focus on your breath.

Quietly recite or chant the mantra *VAM*. You may wish to hold the mantra and repeat several times. Do what feels comfortable.

Chanting the mantra may help you to increase your love for yourself and experience happiness. The mantra may help to increase your positive energy level, creativity, and dispel negative thoughts.

Root Chakra (Muladhara)

located at the base of the spine
The mantra for the Root chakra is LAM.
Element: earth
Energy: survival, fight or flight, instinct, stability
Connected to earth and physical body
Solfeggio Sound Frequency 396Hz
Connect with the colours red and black

The root chakra is where everything begins. This wheel-like chakra is thought to be the foundation on which the entire chakra system is based. Some energy healers say that, in order to balance the other chakra centres, the root chakra must be healed and balanced first. The root chakra is the driving force that gives us the energy to live our daily lives. It is said that the root chakra has deep roots, like those of a tree hidden beneath the earth. The root chakra grounds us, physically and mentally, to the present moment. Herbs that may help balance this chakra include dandelion root, ginger, and sage. These herbs can be taken as a tea or added to other root-based foods, such as carrots, parsnips, and beets. Crystals that may help with balancing the root chakra usually share the same colour traits—deep red tones and earthy brown hues, such as smoky quartz, hematite, obsidian, and red jasper.

MEditation

You may wish to connect with the colour red. Visualize a red candle glowing or visualize red flowers in a field. Remember, you are safe and protected and when other thoughts come, let them go and refocus on your breath.

Begin by focusing on your breath. Breathe in for a count of four, hold for a count of four, breathe out for a count of four, pause for a count of four. Repeat the breathing exercise a few times. As you continue, you may wish to extend the exhale to six and pause for six. You will begin to relax as you focus on your breath.

Quietly recite or chant the mantra *LAM*. You may wish to hold the mantra and repeat several times. Do what feels comfortable.

Chanting the mantra may help to increase your positive energy level, help to centre and balance yourself, and dispel negative thoughts.

Mudras

The history of mudras, hand gestures in the practice of yoga and meditation, dates back a thousand years. Using mudras is a powerful tool for self-care and empowerment. Mudras are an ancient technique that has been practised to balance the flow of energy and *prana* (breath) in our body. According to yogic science, our body is made up of five elements and each of our fingers represents one of those elements:

Air (Vayu) - Index Finger
Fire (Agni) - Thumb
Water (Jal) - Little Finger
Earth (Prithvi) - Ring Finger
Space (Akash) - Middle Finger

I have highlighted some mudras; however, there are many hand gestures you can use when you are meditating.

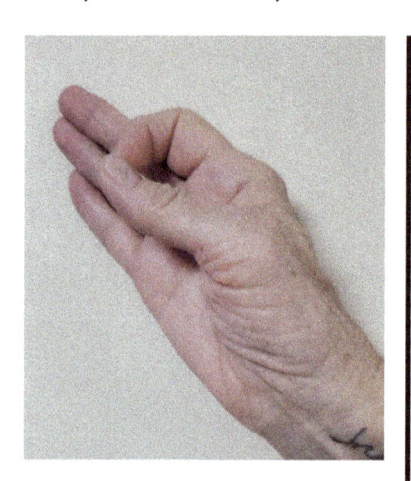

Gyan Mudra

Jnana/Gyan Mudra (Awareness, Knowledge)
The tip of your index finger should touch the tip of your thumb. Straighten the remaining three fingers so that they are relaxed and slightly apart. Now, with the palms facing down, place the hands on the knees.

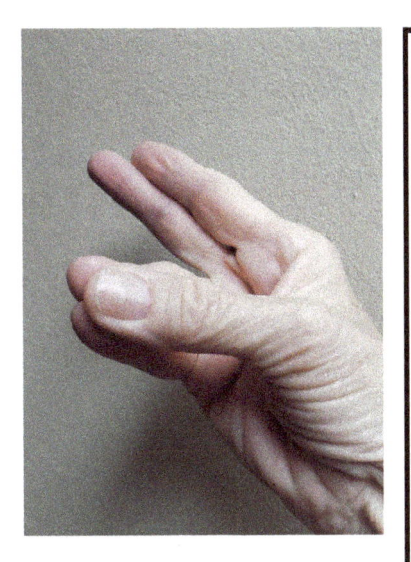

Prana Mudra (Life)
This mudra is for balancing your body, mind, and soul. Gently place the tips of your ring finger and little finger on the tip of your thumb. Straighten the other two fingers, keeping them relaxed and slightly apart. With the palms facing up, place the hands on the knees. Hands and arms should be relaxed.

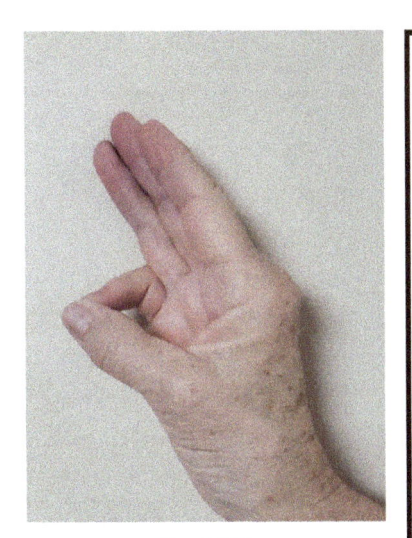

Prana

Buddhi Mudra (mental clarity)
This mudra is performed by touching your thumb to your pinky finger, while holding your other three fingers straight.

Buddhi

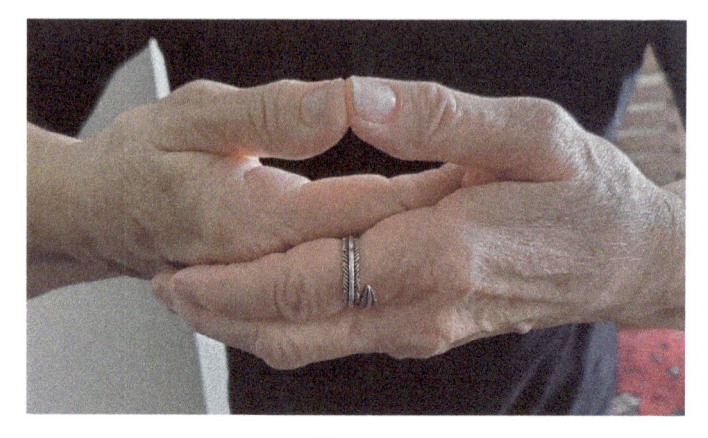

Dhyana

Dhyana (concentration, inner peace)
Your hands facing upward, right hand (enlightenment) rests on top of your left palm (illusion).

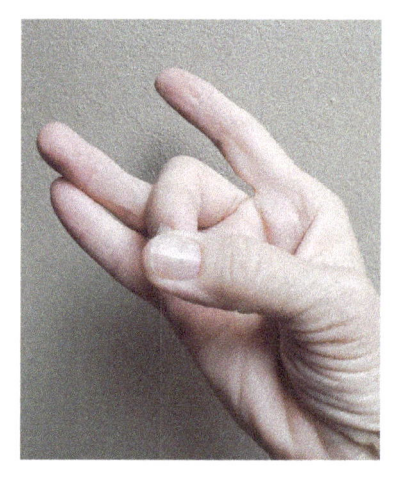

Shuni (or Shoonya) (intuition, alertness)
This mudra is performed by touching the tip of the middle finger to the thumb tip, while keeping the other three fingers straight and relaxed.

Shuni (or Shoonya)

Healing Effects of Tea

Studies have shown there are a variety of teas that will help with health and wellness.

Healing Effects of Tea

Helps to fight off inflammation	Contains antioxidants and polyphenols to help with heart health
May help boost your immune system	Contains less caffeine than coffee
Helps to balance energy levels	Helps with digestion
May help to improve cholesterol levels and lower blood pressure	Helps with calmness and relaxation
Helps with relationships as the focus of the tea ceremony is to help resolve conflicts	Is used for medicinal purposes and has healing properties

Healing Effects of Meditation

Healing Effects of Meditation

Improves focus and attention	Helps to normalize blood pressure and decrease heart rate
Helps to bring harmony to your relationships	Helps to increase energy levels with more efficient oxygen use by the body
Releases emotional turbulence and helps balance emotions by focusing on the breath	Helps to increase level of happiness and change negative thought patterns
Helps to decrease inflammation in the body	Helps to strengthen immunity and reduce production of stress hormones including cortisol and adrenaline
Increases the body's neurotransmitters of well-being (dopamine, serotonin, endorphins)	Promotes relaxation and restful sleep

The Tea Families

There are six main categories of tea from the camellia sinensis plant—white, green, yellow, oolong, black, and pu-erh. Each tea family comes from a particular method of processing the leaves or plant. Tea is created from only one plant and then classified into many different varieties. There are also numerous plants and flowers steeped for their flavours and health benefits.

In addition to the healing teas already mentioned, there are teas that may also help with healing. Your health is vital and herbal teas are not a resource or a substitute to science. Please consult your doctor if you have any side effects.

Herbal

Butterfly Blue Pea tea is rich with antioxidants and may help with blood sugar levels and skin health.

Banana tea may help with sleep.

Chamomile tea may help with relaxation and sleep.

Calendula tea, packed with antioxidants, may help with skin and oral health.

Dandelion tea, a source of potassium and other minerals, may help with blood flow and balancing energy levels.

Ginger tea may help with inflammation.

Hibiscus tea may help with skin health.

Lavender tea may help with relaxation.

Peppermint tea may help with digestion.

Pineapple tea may help with well-being, digestion, strengthening of teeth, and reduction of inflammation (vitamin C, manganese, enzyme bromelain).

Red raspberry tea may help with balancing hormones.

Rooibus tea may help with digestion, skin health, and allergies.

Summertime Savory tea with coriander, cumin, fennel (1 teaspoon each). Steep for eight to ten minutes. May help with digestion and hydration.

Black Tea

English Breakfast: A blend of many black tea leaves grown around the globe, traditionally blended with Keemun (China) and Assam (India) black teas. It tends to be stronger than other teas.

Irish Breakfast: A blend of several black tea leaves, predominately Assam, grown in India. It has a robust and intense flavour.

Darjeeling: Very fine, delicate tea leaves. Darjeeling gardens are grown in the Himalayan foothills, up the mountainside at different elevations, and each harvest tastes distinctly different. The leaves are picked at different times of the year depending upon the monsoon rainfall. It has a fruity aroma.

Pu-erh: Pu-erh is known to help relieve diarrhea and indigestion. It is a tea known for its bitter, earthy taste. To help with the bitterness, it is sometimes blended with other teas and flowers.

Green Teas

Jasmine: The jasmine plant is known for its fragrant flowers. The flowers bloom at night and are picked in the early morning. The flowers are kept in a cool place and, just as they are about to open, they are dried with tea leaves. The tea leaves absorb the jasmine fragrance. Jasmine tea has a balanced, delicate floral taste. Jasmine tea may help to relieve diarrhea.

Matcha: Matcha is a powdered leaf that is dissolved in water rather than infused. It is whisked in boiled water to create a frothy, nourishing beverage. The finest grades are sweet and delicate. The production process consists of picking the young leaves at the top of the plant and finely grinding the whole leaf. Matcha may help with balancing energy levels and general well-being. It may also help to boost your immune system, stimulate metabolism, detoxify, boost your concentration, and lower your cholesterol levels.

Note: The information in this book is intended for educational use only and is not a substitute for professional medical advice, diagnosis, or treatment. Always seek the advice of a physician or other qualified health providers with any questions you may have regarding a medical condition and before undertaking any diet, supplement, fitness, or other health programs.

A Morning Routine

A morning routine is important. A daily activity energizes the mind, soul, and body. Spiritual growth depends on doing spiritual activities, and, in particular, prayer or meditation. One of the most important activities is to get outside and enjoy the sunshine for even a few minutes.

Everyone will have their own spiritual morning routine. *Habit stack* your meditation time with an existing daily habit so you will be reminded to meditate on a regular basis. While you are enjoying a cup of tea, bring out your journal and jot down some inspiring ideas or perhaps a dream, and when your tea is finished, you know it is time to meditate. Set an intention to experience joy and compassion throughout the day. I have started using a *touchstone* at my front door. A touchstone is a small crystal, stone, or object that is a reminder as I enter or leave my home to experience love, compassion, and joy.

Enjoy a cup of tea, journal, and self-reflect for a few minutes.

An Evening Routine

A balanced sleep is important to our emotional health and well-being. Sleep supports our digestive and immune systems. Sleep helps to repair and rejuvenate cells and tissues. It facilitates learning and helps to build neurological pathways. An evening routine is important for sleep. We can turn off our cell phones and allow the body and mind to relax and unwind at night. Think about the routines that will help you release stress and leave unresolved emotions.

Positive affirmations will help restore a balanced sleep cycle. An evening routine can be as simple as repeating positive affirmations as it helps to release the day's activities—e.g., I am calm, I am supported, there is nothing I need to achieve in this moment. An affirmation can help prepare us for the benefits of sleep as well as prepare us for the next day. Sleep helps with our mental health and our ability to fight disease.

An evening prayer that has become important to me is to express *sorrow, to ask for forgiveness, and to express gratitude*. I start by saying I am sorry for the day's events where I felt or experienced something was amiss, perhaps my behaviour did not reflect gratitude, or maybe I was not fully aware of some situations. My next step is to seek forgiveness for any actions or words that may have been unsettling, as well as for past memories. I then express my gratitude for everything and everyone in my life, and finally, I close with love. I do not think it matters who

An Evening Routine

I am forgiving, thanking, or why I am sorry, as I believe the universe has received my prayer. I feel it. And I know there is nothing more powerful than love.

An evening routine is a time to be grateful and to help us heal. It is a time when we connect with our creativity and perhaps gain a better understanding of our purpose.

Set aside a few moments in the evening and allow yourself to explore and reflect on the day's activities. Rest in the presence of the moment and know you are safe and protected. Before you close your eyes and fall into sleep, say a few positive affirmations or phrases that will resonate with you and connect with the universe—e.g., I am joyful, I am confident, I am peaceful, I accomplished today what I set out to do, I experienced what I wanted to experience, I met the person I was meant to meet, I have everything I need right now. Affirmations will help you manifest your goals. Let your affirmations co-create a joy-filled life.

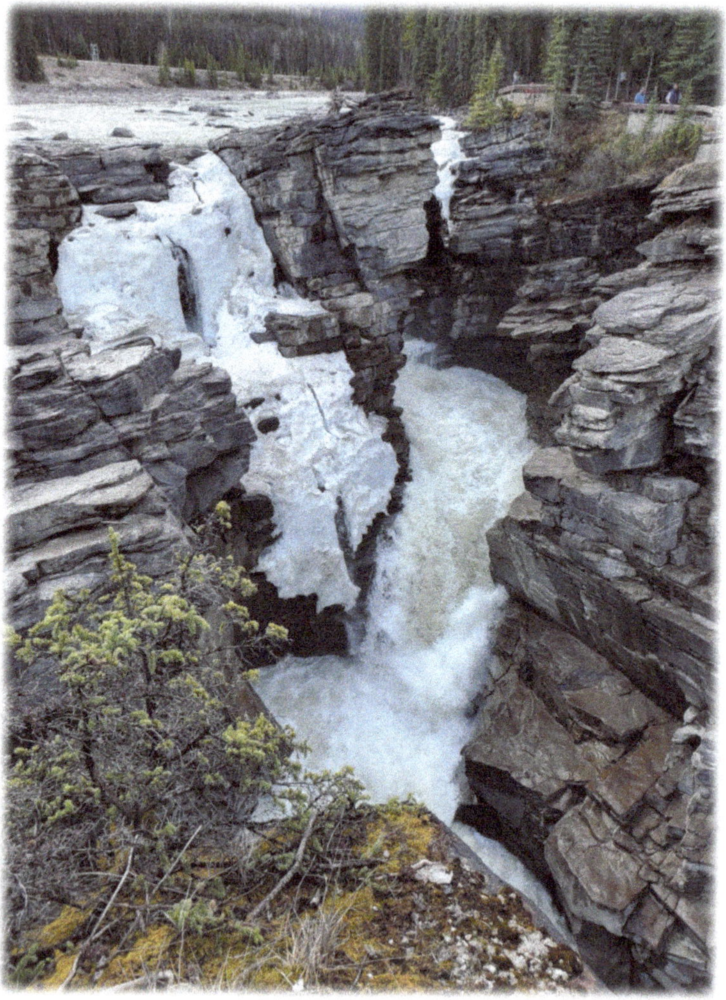

Life Loves Me

I am love
I am light
You are love
You are light
Consciously creating

Me, myself, I
Love invisible
Co-creating with my
Higher Power

You, them, they
Compassion invisible
Co-creating with your
Creator

Love and compassion invisible
Together, the world will survive
Everything will be made known
Everything is as it should be

Maureen Lowden

Life loves us all. Breathe in and say, *Life loves me*. I was given this saying from an earth angel, a friend. As I reflect upon my life I realize that my journey has been about learning. It has been about balancing a spiritual life with a busy daily life. It has been about adjusting, changing, learning, understanding, and teaching. I am never more at peace than when I am listening to the sounds around me and meditating for a better understanding. Meditation is about setting up a ritual where you feel safe, comfortable, and loved. Enjoying a cup of tea is also about establishing a ritual and for a moment life stands still while you consciously sip your tea.

The practice of drinking tea is about starting at the beginning and creating a ritual that you enjoy. Choose your favourite mug or cup. Then choose the tea. There is really no right or wrong way to enjoy tea. It is what feels right for you and when it is the right time for you. Keep your tea in a special container, perhaps one you enjoy looking at and that brings to mind a favourite memory. Boil the water to the temperature for your chosen tea and let the tea steep for a few minutes for optimal flavour. While you are waiting, choose the milk and sweetener you like, perhaps a favourite spoon, and a cookie or two. Set your intention, and then sit down. Set aside some time for mindful reflection and be present in the moment.

Engage your senses. Watch a flower unfold or the leaves swirling around in the teapot or in your cup. Feel the warmth coming from the teapot and your mug. Smell the aroma being created by the blending of ingredients. Sip your tea consciously, enjoying every sip and feeling it warm or cool your body as it travels down your throat. Know that your hands are holding something special and that your body will feel the benefits. Enjoy and take a moment to relax and unwind. Visualize a beautiful sunset or sunrise. Enjoy the colours that you see—pink, red, blue, white. Visualize the Northern Lights dancing across the sky or big, white, puffy, cumulus clouds carrying your worries away for a few moments. Allow Tea & MEditation to bring your mind, body, soul, and spirit into balance.

Namaste. Shanti. Shalom, Shalom. Blessings.

There is always time for Tea & MEditation.

M. Lowden

Mindful Awareness

A short meditation to help balance your energy and relieve stress.

Find a comfortable position. Take a few deep breaths. Feel your chest rising and falling with each breath. Envision your breath flowing to your heart and then out through your toes and out through the top of your head. Breathe in deeply. Establish a relaxing breathing pattern. Feel the stress leaving your body. Lower and relax your shoulders and relax your neck muscles. Relax your facial muscles and, now, smile. Feel the joy your smile brings and let the feeling of joy travel throughout your body. Be conscious of the awareness of joy in your whole body.

Pour yourself a cup of tea, take a sip, and become aware of its warmth and healing properties. Enjoy the moment.

Accommodating the Water - A Taoist Parable

As the story goes, an old man was walking along a river bank. To his side powerful river rapids flowed furiously leading to a steep and plummeting waterfall. Suddenly the man stumbled, fell into the river rapids and was swept up by the force of the current. Onlookers watched with horror, fearing for the man's life as he was carried downstream and flung over the edge of the waterfall. People rushed to the edge of the cliff and peered down through the mist to learn of the man's fate. To their astonishment, standing on the rocky banks at the bottom of the falls was the man smiling and unharmed. People asked him how he managed to survive his fall. He replied, *Without thinking, I allowed myself to be shaped by the water. Plunging into the waterfall, I let go of any tension and thoughts and allowed the water to carry me.*

Go with the flow.

Let go of any thoughts and emotions, allow yourself to be shaped with the right viewpoint, and see things the way they truly are.

The unstoppable spirit of renewal is in you. Trust it. Learn that it flows through you and all of life."

Jack Kornfield

Wrapping It Up

Meditation can just be living your life – by starting your day with the intention to be joyful and grateful. Can we do this journey alone? Maybe. It is good to have times throughout the day when you are alone and silent and to offer thanks. I think we can experience life to its fullest by being alone and by being in community – and to ask for help. Our greatest learning usually comes from being in community and developing and learning from relationships. Our greatest ability in community is to listen and understand without evaluating or judging. What is being expressed? Is it the best time to offer advice or express an opinion when asked? Is there a better way to respond? What is your intuition relaying to you? Spirit can be found in everything. The Divine and Spirit are in nature, your workplace, within you, in the very nature of the planet. Do you hear the question? Do you hear the answer?

Enjoying a cup of tea may bring warm, cozy memories of home. A cup of tea can be enjoyed alone, with friends, and with a group of people. The intention is important. Be conscious of the drink in your hand. Be conscious of the memories and feelings that come with each sip and smell. What comes to mind? What do you see? Do you hear the question? Do you hear the answer?

Love is our strength, compassion, and grace. We need love to be the lens that we look through to find the truth and to find our way in living life on this planet. Love is the way, the truth, and the light. It is the only way and the only answer.

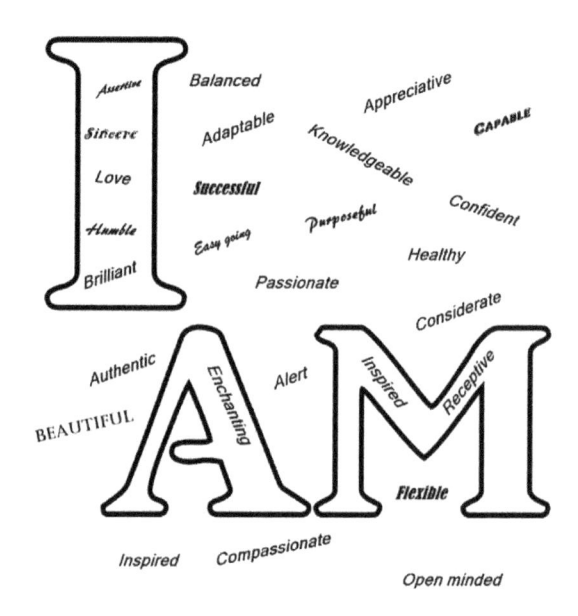

I AM

Assertive, Balanced, Appreciative, Capable, Sincere, Adaptable, Knowledgeable, Love, Successful, Confident, Humble, Easy going, Purposeful, Healthy, Brilliant, Passionate, Considerate, Authentic, Enchanting, Alert, Inspired, Receptive, Beautiful, Flexible, Inspired, Compassionate, Open minded

31 Days of Meditation

Consistent meditation is important to achieve the results you desire, e.g., better sleep, reducing anxiety, or an understanding and connection with your Higher Power. Perhaps using this chart will help you to see some consistency in your efforts to establish a meditation practice.

1	2	3	4	5	6	7
8	9	10	11	12	13	14
15	16	17	18	19	20	21
22	23	24	25	26	27	28
29	30	31				

> Lokah Samastah Sukhino Bhavantu
>
> May all beings everywhere be happy and free, and may the thoughts, words, and actions of my own life contribute in some way to that happiness and to the freedom for all.
>
> Lokah Samastah Sukhino Bhavantu is a beautiful Sanskrit mantra that is often used as a prayer of love for the world around us.

Acknowledgements

Thank you to my sister, Cheryl Upfold, for her never-ending support. Thank you to my brother-in-law for his patience and support so my sister could spend many hours reading and editing this attempt at my first book. Thank you to my husband and brother and all those around me who have supported me throughout my years on this planet. I wish to acknowledge my mother and father, grandparents, aunts and uncles, and all my ancestors for the life they forged on this planet as they persevered through hardships, wars, famine, losses, and racism, and became stronger for it.

A special hug goes to my daughter and my grandchildren, who I am always thinking about, love dearly, and for whom I pray daily for their many questions (present and future) and for their choices in life. Sometimes we are so wrapped up in the questions that we do not hear the answers and need to step back from doing and breathe.

Thank you to the many teachers guiding me on my spiritual path. Thank you to all the tea drinkers in my life and for the spiritual conversations. Thank you to friends. Thank you to all the teachers before me and those whom I meet with weekly for their immense knowledge of energy, the universe, and the Divine. Thank you to everyone helping me to learn valuable lessons for my personal and spiritual growth, and to hone in on my weaknesses and my strengths.

Thank you to pastors, Robyn Elliot and Marc Gagnon, the leaders, and the people at Lakeside Church, Guelph, Ontario, Canada, for their kindness and warmth and helping me to change how I tell my stories. Thank you to our daughter for the many opportunities to learn and for the love she has shown. I realized I needed to give gratitude for all the people and influences in my life—to change the pain into a gain. Healing pain and trauma is to finally come to peace with the *not being able to make sense of it*. Perhaps there is no right or wrong; it is learning that pain is a gift that can open the door to knowing your true self just a little better.

I would like to note here that I am not an editor of books. As an elementary school teacher perfection was not a goal I taught but doing your best was considered to be the paramount version of success. As I was writing this book, I began to realize that I do not have the monetary funds to edit this book to perfection. It will be published, I am sure, with mistakes for which I apologize. My intention when I began writing the book was to help me understand meditation and my love of tea a little bit better. This has been accomplished and will be a lifelong practice.

To everyone, as well as myself, I send my love and pray for healing and joy. I have learned that we must love the whole person—those in your tribe who fit well with your beliefs and you hold love and space for in your thoughts, those who have caused deep pain, for those who do not fit into your tribe, and for those you do not know yet.

Questions are good. Never stop questioning and allow any answers that come to you to sit softly on your heart and then let them go. The universe hears you and, while you may not get the answers you expected, it will provide you with choices and the awareness you will need to help you on this life journey.

Acknowledgements

Sometimes it falls apart before it comes together.

Colette Baron-Reid

*I am not my old story. I am not any trauma.
I am new and beautiful every day. I am seizing the day!*

Karen Ruimy

Become a vibrational match to that which you desire.

Unknown

*Many Blessings.
Shalom, shalom.
Namaste.*

Books, teachers, and references

The Republic of Tea, *The Book of Tea & Herbs*, The Cole Group, Santa Rosa, CA., 1993.

Dr. Masaru Emoto, *Hidden Messages in Water*. Atria Books, Beyond Words Publishing Inc., 20827. N.W. Cornell Rd. (2005).

Kevin Gascoyne, François Marchand, Jasmin Desharnais & Hugo Américi, *Tea, History Terroirs Varieties*, 3rd Edition 2021.

NIV Women's Devotional Bible, New International Version, Zondervan Publishing House

Joey Wargachuk, *Chakra and crystal healer practitioner*, Wargachuk Academy, Calgary, Alberta, 2022.

Journal Prompts & Self-Reflection Questions: There is so much information from ancestral knowledge to present day that it is difficult to acknowledge or cite one person. I acknowledge all teaching masters who have gone before me.

Affirmations: There is so much information from ancestral knowledge to present day that it is difficult to acknowledge or cite one person. I acknowledge all teaching masters who have gone before me.

Intentions: There is so much information from ancestral knowledge to present day that it is difficult to acknowledge or cite one person. I acknowledge all teaching masters who have gone before me.

Tea & MEditation: There is so much information from ancient and ancestral knowledge to present day that it is difficult to acknowledge or cite one person. I acknowledge all teaching masters who have gone before me.

Photo Credits

All photos unless otherwise noted have been taken by the author.

Art Graphics

OhsoLively Digital Graphics, Etsy

Justpicturethis, Etsy

Printed in the USA
CPSIA information can be obtained
at www.ICGtesting.com
JSHW071508060924
69264JS00014B/95